English Mistakes
Italians ~~Do~~ Make

Paul Andrew Jarvis

Contents

INTRODUCTION

English Mistakes Italians Make has been designed as a practical learning tool for students of all levels from Pre-Intermediate to Advanced, and a resource book for teachers wishing to focus on specific language areas. As well as a classification of grammatical, syntactical, lexical, spelling and pronunciation errors typically made by Italian learners, it provides suggested corrections and, where appropriate, a brief analysis and/or advice on learning strategies. Given that many mistakes can be categorised in more than one way, cross-referencing has been introduced to allow students to compare and contrast related language items.

Each chapter is supplemented with exercises that are suitable for both self-study purposes and classroom use. Keys for these exercises, including sample answers for open-ended questions, are supplied.

The mistakes listed in the book are real examples* collected by the author from a number of sources in the course of the last five years, most notably the spoken and written English of students and colleagues at the University of Bari and the Polytechnic of Bari, but also the language used by Italian friends and acquaintances, the press, the media and businesses, and – last but not least – by the current prime minister of Italy, Mr Matteo Renzi.

For practical purposes, other mistakes not relevant to the category in which each example has been included have been eliminated.

PART 1: MISTAKES, CORRECTIONS & EXERCISES

Classics

1) I <u>am</u> born in a small village near Foggia.
I was born in a small village near Foggia.

2) It was a fantastic <u>travel</u>.
It was a fantastic trip/holiday.
"Travel" is an uncountable noun and as such cannot be used with "a".

3) I <u>like very much the art</u>.
I like art very much.
Avoid separating the verb and the object. See the chapter Word Order.

4) My family <u>is composed by four members</u>.
There are four people in my family.

5) I'd like to <u>do the</u> teacher.
I'd like to be a teacher.
See the chapter Do & Make *for further examples.*

6) I'm <u>attending</u> a <u>master</u>.
I'm doing a master's [course]. / I'm doing a training course.
A "master" is a person who is highly accomplished in a particular field ("Hemingway was a master of the short sentence"), not a course of study. Note that a "master's" is usually a one or two-year academic degree course – typically, it is taken after a Bachelor's degree and before a PhD – while a "training course" tends to be more practical/vocational and can range in length from one or two days to several years.

7) The food was <u>so and so</u>.
The food was mediocre / nothing special / so-so.
English speakers use "so-so" much less frequently than Italian speakers use "così così". The best strategy for language students is probably to avoid it. Note that "so-and-so" is a noun used variously to refer to a non-specific person (often translatable with "Pinco Pallino") or to a rude or annoying person.

8) He hates <u>staying</u> without his phone.
He hates being without his phone.
In the vast majority of cases, the Italian verb "stare" is translated with the verb "to be", not "to stay". See also 32) and 33) in the chapter Wrong Word.

9) I <u>knew</u> her during a trip to Rome.

I met her during a trip to Rome. / I got to know her during a trip to Rome.

In this kind of situation "met" gives the idea that the two people were introduced, or introduced themselves, to each other; "got to know" suggests an acquaintance developing over time.

10) We came <u>with the car</u>.

We came by car. / We came in the car. / We drove here.

11) <u>In this</u> moment I don't know.

At the moment I don't know.

12) <u>Hello</u>! <u>We see</u> next week.

Goodbye/Bye! See you next week.

See also 49) in the chapter Wrong Word.

13) Thank you for <u>all</u>!

Thank you for everything!

14) <u>According to me</u>, Messi is even better than Maradona was.

In my opinion, Messi is even better than Maradona was. / If you ask me, Messi is even better than Maradona was.

"According to..." is most frequently used with the third person ("According to a government spokesman..."; "According to her..."; etc), occasionally with the second person ("Well, according to you, it wasn't even going to rain!"), and practically never with the first person. Note that "If you ask me..." is informal.

15) I suggest you to read this book.

I suggest [that] you read this book.

16) I think <u>yes</u>.

I think so.

Note that the negative equivalent is "I don't think so". The expression "I think not" has a similar meaning but is usually facetious.

17) Thanks to my job, I had the <u>possibility</u> to travel and meet people from all over the world.

Thanks to my job, I had the opportunity/chance to travel and meet people from all over the world.

18) Last summer I worked <u>in a camping</u>.

Last summer I worked on/at a camp-site.

The noun "camping" is uncountable and denotes the activity, not the place ("Camping in England can often be a nightmare"). See also 66) in the chapter Wrong Word.

19) It was a <u>beautiful</u> party!

It was a great party!

The word "beautiful" is used much less frequently in English than the term "bello" in Italian. It is generally employed to emphasise specifically aesthetic qualities ("those flowers are beautiful"; "she's a beautiful woman"; "What a beautiful painting!"; etc) and not simply to express a positive opinion about something ("he's a nice person"; "it was a marvellous match"; "was the film good?"; etc).

20) She <u>is graduated</u> in music.

She has a degree in music. / She is a music graduate.

Note also the following forms: "She graduated in music last year" and "She has just graduated in music". See also 1) and 2) in the chapter Tenses – Present Perfect & Past Perfect.

EXERCISES

A. Underline the most appropriate word or phrase in each sentence:

1) He *am / is / was / were* born in London.

2) In my family *are / is / we are / there are* five people.

3) When I finish school I'd like to *do the / do a / be the / be a* teacher.

4) I'm *attending / making / doing / frequenting* a master's.

5) I suggest *them to ask / them ask / they asking / they ask* an expert.

6) I have *a degree / a graduate / graduation* in engineering.

7) Thank you *for all / for everything / of all / of everything*!

8) Where did you and your girlfriend *know / knew / meet / met*?

9) He is on the phone *in this moment / at the moment / in the moment / at that moment*.

10) We spent our holiday at a *camping / camp / camper / camp-site*.

11) The holiday was great but the food was *discreet / so-and-so / nothing special / medium* .

B. Write answers to the following questions, then ask the questions to your study partner and make a note of his/her answers:

1) Where were you born?

2) How many people are there in your family?

3) What kind of job would you most like to do?

4) Where is your favourite camp-site?

5) How big a problem would being without your phone be for you?

6) How do you usually get to work/university/school?

7) How did you meet your best friend?

8) Which parts of Italy do you suggest foreign tourists visit first?

9) Have you ever done a training course?

Adjectives

1) <u>All</u> morning I wake up at seven o'clock.
Every morning I wake up at seven o'clock.

2) Not <u>very</u> people know about her.
Not many people know about her.
"Very" is occasionally used immediately before a noun in the sense of "very same" ("this is the very room in which she wrote her novels") but never in the sense of "molti/molte".

3) <u>Every person</u> knows that.
Everyone/Everybody knows that.

4) <u>In every case</u>, I need more time to finish this.
In any case, I need more time to finish this.
See also 11) in the chapter Some & Any.

5) My father is a very <u>simple</u> man.
My father is a very uncomplicated/straightforward/down-to-earth/unpretentious man.
When used to describe a person, the adjective "simple" suggests very limited mental capacity.

6) I have long <u>and</u> brown hair and small <u>and</u> brown eyes.
I have long, brown hair and small, brown eyes.
Two adjectives preceding a noun are generally joined by a comma. See also 7) below.

7) I was born in a small <u>and</u> pretty town called Locorotondo.
I was born in a small, pretty town called Locorotondo.

8) It is the most <u>touristic</u> of the islands.
It is the most touristy of the islands.
Note that "touristy" has a negative connotation ("It's too touristy here!"). In other contexts "turistico" is translated with "tourist" ("tourist menu"; "tourist resort") or "tour" ("tour guide").

9) The story is set in England in <u>the first 19th century</u>.
The story is set in England in the early 19th century.

10) The novel is still very <u>present</u> today.

The novel is still very relevant today.

11) My mum says I should not wear heels because I am <u>high</u>.

My mum says I should not wear heels because I am tall.

When used to describe a person, the adjective "high" describes the euphoric state induced by, for example, marijuana.

12) It is a very <u>particular</u> story.

It is a very unusual story.

13) I like December very much because of the <u>big</u> number of presents I receive every year.

I like December very much because of the large number of presents I receive every year.

14) I developed a <u>big</u> passion for belly-dancing.

I developed a great passion for belly-dancing.

15) There is a <u>great</u> terrace at the front and a small terrace at the back.

There is a large terrace at the front and a small terrace at the back.

16) This is a <u>strong</u> example of what I mean.

This is a good / an excellent example of what I mean.

See also 31) in the chapter Collocations.

17) We have been <u>engaged</u> since primary school.

We have been together since primary school.

The English term "engaged" is more specific than the Italian "fidanzato": it means that the couple have decided to marry and suggests that arrangements for the wedding are being made.

18) I really enjoyed the holiday. It was <u>very funny</u>.

I really enjoyed the holiday. It was great fun.

Distinguish "fun", which can be a noun (usually translated by "divertimento") or an adjective ("divertente", in the general sense) from "funny", which is an adjective that is used either to describe something or someone that makes people laugh ("Woody Allen is a funny guy") or describing something or someone strange ("It has a funny taste"). See also 19) below.

19) I spent a lot of time riding my bicycle; it was <u>so funny</u>!
I spent a lot of time riding my bicycle; it was such fun / great fun!

20) A *trullo* is a very <u>characteristic</u> building.
A trullo is a very distinctive building.

21) The soundtrack is very <u>suggestive</u>.
The soundtrack is very evocative/haunting/atmospheric.

22) I'm <u>realist</u> and <u>optimist</u>.
I'm realistic and optimistic. / I'm a realist and an optimist.
"Realist" and "optimist" are nouns.

23) I prefer a <u>philosophic</u> approach.
I prefer a philosophical approach.

24) She can't stand <u>classic</u> music.
She can't stand classical music.

25) It's just <u>poetical</u> licence.
It's just poetic licence.

26) Italy has serious <u>economical</u> problems.
Italy has serious economic problems.
The term "economical" is most often used to describe something which is efficient or cheap to run ("an economical car"; "an economical heating system").

27) It is <u>rich</u> of history.
It is full of history.

28) She is a very <u>quite</u> person.
She is a very quiet/calm/relaxed person.
Note that when used of a person the term "quiet" is more limited than the Italian "tranquillo"; it describes someone who doesn't speak, or isn't speaking, very much.

EXERCISES

A. Rearrange the letters provided to form a suitable adjective to fill each gap:

1) She has a siesta _____ afternoon from three till four. (YVEER)

2) He isn't pretentious at all! He's the most _____ person you could wish to meet. (NWOD-OT-HATER)

3) My wife is working that day so we wouldn't be able to go to the wedding in _____ case. (YAN)

4) I don't like the place: it's full of souvenir shops and too _____ ! (SOIRYUTT)

5) It was invented in the _____ twentieth century. (RAYLE)

6) Although it is five hundred years old, the story is still _____ today. (ETRLNAVE)

7) Gaudi's architecture is extremely _____ .(SULANUU)

8) The hotel has a very _____ style. (SCEVITINDIT)

9) This is an _____ example of late Impressionist art. (TELECLENX)

10) You should try it! It's a _____ way to learn. (UFN)

11) I love this music: it's really _____ . (GHUNTIAN)

12) It's very difficult to see an end to the current _____ crisis. (ONICCEMO)

B. Write answers to the following questions, then ask the questions to your study partner and make a note of his/her answers:

1) What are the things you do every morning?

2) How touristy is the place where you live?

3) What is the most distinctive building in your town?

4) Have you heard any funny jokes recently?

5) What is the most haunting piece of music you know?

6) How often do you listen to classical music?

7) Do you think of yourself as an optimistic or pessimistic person?

8) Is there anyone in your family you would describe as quiet?

9) Have you had any unusual experiences recently?

10) Who is the most down-to-earth person you know?

Adverbs

1) I've read <u>quite</u> everything by this author.
I've read almost everything by this author.

2) It is <u>much</u> expensive.
It is very expensive.
"Much" is used to translate "molto" before certain adjectives that are also past participles ("much loved"; "much talked about"; etc). See also 3) below. "Very" translates "molto" before other adjectives.

3) She was <u>very</u> criticised for this.
She was much criticised for this.

4) I was <u>very</u> amazed.
I was absolutely amazed.
Avoid "very" with ungradable adjectives such as "perfect", "unique" and "incredulous". In these cases we often use adverbs like "absolutely", "quite" (in the sense of "absolutely") and "totally". See also 5) below.

5) It was a <u>very</u> fantastic experience.
It was an absolutely fantastic experience.

6) Everybody has problems, <u>also</u> kings and queens.
Everybody has problems, even kings and queens.
When "anche" is used in the sense of "persino", it is usually translated with "even".

7) <u>Also if</u> I don't want to, I study at the weekend.
Even if I don't want to, I study at the weekend.
"Anche se" is translated "even if" or "even though" depending on the context. See also 9) in the chapter Conjunctions.

8) He has <u>no more</u> long hair.
He no longer has long hair. / He doesn't have long hair any more.

9) During my teens I travelled <u>so much</u> with my parents and my brothers.

During my teens I travelled a great deal / a lot with my parents and my brothers.

The English term "so much" is considerably less versatile than the Italian "tanto/tantissimo". It is occasionally used in exclamations ("I love her so much!") but more frequently with "...that" ("I travelled so much that I got bored of it").

10) Luckily <u>it's gone all good</u>.

Luckily it has all gone well. / Luckily it all went well.

11) This is one of my favourite films, starring two of the best actors <u>in circulation</u>.

This is one of my favourite films, starring two of the best actors around.

12) I have known her <u>since always</u>.

I have known her for as long as I can remember.

13) <u>In a first time</u> I wanted to study chemistry.

At first I wanted to study chemistry.

14) My father has <u>ever</u> loved my mother.

My father has always loved my mother.

"Ever" is only used to translate "sempre" in expressions such as "for ever" ("forever" in American English) and in poetic language ("It was ever thus").

15) His mornings are spent <u>in loneliness</u>.

His mornings are spent alone. / His mornings are lonely.

"Lonely" and "loneliness" refer to the emotion caused by solitude ("He often feels lonely"; "Loneliness is a terrible thing"). "Alone" simply indicates that nobody else is present.

16) The holiday was <u>too much short</u>.

The holiday was too short.

"Too much" is never used to qualify adjectives or adverbs though it may be used with nouns ("too much noise"; "too much traffic"). See also 17) and 18) below.

17) I was <u>too much timid</u> to speak.

I was too timid/shy to speak.

18) She speaks <u>too much quickly</u>.

She speaks too quickly.

19) I like it because it is <u>too beautiful</u>.

I like it because it is very/extremely beautiful.

The term "too" nearly always has a negative connotation. Exceptions tend to be idiomatic phrases such as "too wonderful for words".

20) It depends on <u>how much you are ready</u>.

It depends on how ready you are.

21) I've never had <u>a so bad feeling</u>.

I've never had such a bad feeling.

22) We have never seen <u>so quick changes</u>.

We have never seen such quick changes.

23) I, or <u>better</u> my department, paid €180 for it.

I, or rather my department, paid €180 for it.

24) <u>Sincerely</u>, I don't agree with you.

To be honest, I don't agree with you.

25) These are described <u>under</u>.

These are described below.

26) There are some <u>buildings very important for their architecture</u>.

There are some very architecturally important buildings.

27) In recent years this has been one of the <u>most discussed</u> subjects.

In recent years this has been one of the most widely discussed subjects.

28) I <u>absolutely</u> recommend this book to everyone.

I highly recommend this book to everyone.

EXERCISES

A. Correct each sentence by replacing one word with the alternative provided:

1) We spent quite all the money we had. (ALMOST)

2) Parachuting is much dangerous. (VERY)

3) Matera is very unique. (ABSOLUTELY)

4) The film has been very talked about. (MUCH)

5) We're going to go out for a walk also if it rains. (EVEN)

6) – Did you enjoy the holiday?   – So much! (VERY)

7) You really should read this article. It's too interesting! (EXTREMELY)

8) Everything went good. (WELL)

9) We have ever lived in this house. (ALWAYS)

10) It cost me, or better my father, a lot of money. (RATHER)

B. Give examples of:

1) things that have gone well for you so far this year;

2) something extremely beautiful;

3) an occasion when you were too shy to speak;

4) a possession you have had for as long as you can remember;

5) someone you know who speaks too quickly;

6) a problem that even rich people have;

7) an absolutely fantastic experience you have had;

8) a possession you no longer have.

Almost!

1) I'll be the happiest <u>women</u> in the world.
I'll be the happiest woman in the world.

2) Do you want <u>smashed</u> potatoes with the fish?
Do you want mashed potatoes with the fish?

3) What are your <u>planes</u> this evening?
What are your plans this evening?

4) A clairvoyant predicts that Hercules will defeat Zeus when the <u>plants</u> are aligned.
A clairvoyant predicts that Hercules will defeat Zeus when the planets are aligned.

5) I <u>felt</u> in love as soon as I saw her.
I fell in love as soon as I saw her.

6) It was a very <u>fanny</u> film.
It was a very funny film.

7) Writing is a <u>mean</u> of preserving and communicating knowledge.
Writing is a means of preserving and communicating knowledge.

8) I read a very interesting book <u>titled</u> "The Book Thief".
I read a very interesting book entitled "The Book Thief".

9) There is an unexpected happy <u>end</u>.
There is an unexpected happy ending.

10) I <u>jointed</u> the local basketball team.
I joined the local basketball team.

11) She is a true romantic <u>heroin</u>.
She is a true romantic heroine.
"Heroin" is a drug.

12) I fell in love with one of my swimming <u>poll</u> friends.
I fell in love with one of my swimming pool friends.

13) At <u>crush</u> hour the train is very full.
At rush hour the train is very full.

14) She cooks better <u>that</u> me.
She cooks better than me.

EXERCISES

A. Correct each sentence by changing, adding or removing just one letter:
1) Woman are generally better than men at this kind of thing.
2) Do you prefer roast potatoes or smashed?
3) What are her planes for the future?
4) There are eight major plants in the solar system.
5) He felt off his bike while he was riding to school.
6) Everyone else was laughing but I didn't think it was fanny.
7) The end doesn't always justify the mean.
8) She jointed the Communist party when she was a student.
9) There is no heroin to compare with Elizabeth Bennet.
10) Unfortunately the hotel didn't have a swimming poll.
11) I feel better that before.

B. Write answers to the following questions, then ask the questions to your study partner and make a note of his/her answers:
1) Have you seen any funny films recently?
2) What are your plans for the weekend?
3) How old were you when you first fell in love?
4) How important are happy endings for you in books and films?
5) Do you ever have problems travelling at rush hour?
6) Have you ever thought of joining a political party?
7) Do you think that the end ever justifies the means?

Class-shifting

1) My parents had already been married for ten years before my <u>arrive</u>.

My parents had already been married for ten years before my arrival.

"Arrive" is a verb, not a noun.

2) Last year I went to <u>French</u> on holiday.

Last year I went to France on holiday.

"French" is most often found as an adjective ("the French Riviera"; "French resistance fighters"; "French onion soup"); as a noun it can refer to the language ("Do you speak French?") or the people ("The French don't like speaking English") but not the country.

3) The protagonist is Guido, a <u>Jewish</u>.

The protagonist is Guido, a Jew.

"Jewish" is an adjective, not a noun.

4) The portrait is very <u>truly</u>.

The portrait is very true. / The portrait is very true to life.

"Truly" is an adverb, not an adjective.

5) She meets another handsome <u>young</u> and agrees to his proposal of marriage.

She meets another handsome young man and agrees to his proposal of marriage.

"Young" is most commonly used as an adjective. It can be used as a plural noun with reference to animals ("Most wild creatures are very protective of their young") or, more occasionally, to people ("This is a problem for young and old alike").

6) At the end of the war, he <u>outs</u> from the camp.

At the end of the war, he escapes from the camp. / At the end of the war, he gets out of the camp.

"Out" is an adverb; it is occasionally used as a verb but not in the sense intended here.

7) I am the <u>responsible</u> of the group.

I am responsible for the group. / I am in charge of the group.

"Responsible" is an adjective, not a noun.

8) I guess I was never destined to be at my <u>easy</u> in this world.

I guess I was never destined to be at my ease in this world.

"Easy" is an adjective, not a noun.

9) We had to deal with some <u>unforeseen</u>.

We had to deal with some unforeseen circumstances.

"Unforeseen" is an adjective, not a noun.

10) I am a great <u>passionate</u> of thrillers.

I am a great fan of thrillers.

"Passionate" is an adjective, not a noun.

11) The <u>fast</u> of the dialogues was a problem: I didn't understand a lot.

The speed of the dialogues was a problem: I didn't understand a lot.

In the sense intended here, "fast" is an adjective, not a noun. As a noun, it means "digiuno".

12) I'm satisfied with my <u>choose</u>.

I'm satisfied with my choice.

"Choose" is a verb, not a noun.

13) During my <u>teenage</u> I discovered an interest in literature.

During my teenage years / my adolescence I discovered an interest in literature.

"Teenage" is an adjective.

14) People say that I'm <u>controversy</u>.

People say that I'm argumentative.

"Controversy" is a noun; the adjective "controversial" describes a person who inspires strong, contrasting opinions ("Tsipras is a controversial figure"), not his/her own tendency to always dispute what others say. It can also be used to describe things.

15) I am a <u>voluntary</u> in a local association that helps immigrants.

I am a volunteer in a local association that helps immigrants.

"Voluntary" is an adjective ("She does a lot of voluntary work").

16) I'm not interested in <u>politic</u>.

I'm not interested in politics.

"Politic" is an adjective; it is rarely used.

17) My parents separated and I moved with my mother to Puglia, where all my <u>familiars</u> live.

My parents separated and I moved with my mother to Puglia, where all my relatives live.

"Familiar" is an adjective ("Who is that lady over there? She looks familiar").

18) In 2011 we visited the <u>southern</u> of Holland.

In 2011 we visited the south of Holland. / In 2011 we visited southern Holland.

"Southern" is an adjective, not a noun.

19) My <u>really</u> dream is to become an actress.

My real dream is to become an actress.

"Really" is an adverb ("It's really cold today"), not an adjective.

20) I used to play <u>everyday</u> in my free time.

I used to play every day in my free time.

"Everyday" is an adjective ("everyday problems"; "everyday expenses"; etc).

EXERCISES

A. Complete each sentence with a word formed from the stem provided:

1) You can pay on _____ or when you leave. (ARRIVE)

2) I am _____ sorry about what happened. (TRUE)

3) They say that _____ and Italian mothers have a lot in common. (JEW)

4) I never feel at _____ in the company of people like that. (EASY)

5) It was a very difficult _____ to make. (CHOOSE)

6) The judges' decision was highly _____ . (CONTROVERSY)

7) A number of _____ helped the local people to clear up after the flooding. (VOLUNTARY)

8) They have been travelling around _____ Italy for several weeks. (SOUTH)

B. Write answers to the following questions, then ask the questions to your study partner and make a note of his/her answers:

1) Have you ever been in charge of anything?

2) How satisfied are you with the choices you have made in life?

3) Where do most of your relatives live?

4) Have you ever worked as a volunteer?

5) On a scale of 1 to 10, how argumentative are you?

6) What do/will you remember most about your adolescence?

7) When did you last have to deal with problems caused by "unforeseen circumstances"?

Collocations

1) My father met my mother at <u>a common friend</u>'s party.

My father met my mother at a mutual friend's party.

When used of a person, the adjective "common" often has a negative connotation; it suggests vulgarity and lack of refinement.

2) He decided to <u>restructure the old house</u>.

He decided to renovate the old house.

The verb "to restructure" is generally used in an abstract rather than a concrete sense, for example to refer to an organisation or to a business ("A number of jobs were lost as a result of restructuring").

3) To <u>gain a bit of money</u>, I <u>distribute flyers</u> at local festivals.

To earn a bit of money, I hand out flyers at local festivals.

Particularly in spoken English, native speakers tend to prefer shorter (often phrasal) verbs like "hand out" to longer (often Latin-derived) alternatives such as "distribute".

4) If all goes according to plan, I will find <u>a safe job</u>.

If all goes according to plan, I will find a secure job.

5) <u>I'm secure it will</u> be fantastic.

I'm sure it will be fantastic.

6) <u>This educational way</u> is considered unorthodox by the boys' parents.

This educational approach is considered unorthodox by the boys' parents.

7) <u>The final of the story</u> surprised me.

The ending of the story surprised me.

As a noun, "final" is usually limited to sporting contexts ("Nadal beat Federer in the final").

8) I've <u>reached some good results</u>.

I've achieved some good results.

9) I have <u>a strong interest in</u> books.

I have a keen interest in books.

10) - I went to Holland for the weekend. - <u>Business or happiness</u>?
- I went to Holland for the weekend. - Business or pleasure?

11) For my seventh birthday, <u>my parents gifted me</u> a Nintendo 64.
For my seventh birthday, my parents gave me a Nintendo 64.
The verb "to gift" means to give something unintentionally, usually to your own detriment ("The Arsenal goalkeeper gifted Tottenham a crucial goal"; "By squabbling among themselves, the Left gifted victory to the Right").

12) I <u>lived some special moments</u> with this person.
I had some special times with this person.
See also 6) and 7) in the chapter Transitive or Intransitive.

13) <u>This brought me to take</u> a difficult decision.
This led me to take a difficult decision.

14) <u>The audience is captured</u> by the dialogues.
The audience is captivated by the dialogues.
A person who is "captured" is arrested or taken prisoner.

15) I <u>used to read enough</u> every afternoon after school.
I used to read quite a lot every afternoon after school.
"Enough" gives the idea of sufficiently for an explicit or implicit purpose ("I read enough to keep my teacher happy"; "It doesn't rain enough in the desert").

16) I've also tried to <u>expand my cultural baggage</u>.
I've also tried to broaden my cultural horizons/awareness.

17) I attended <u>a theatre laboratory</u>.
I attended a theatre workshop.

18) This has caused <u>big damage</u> to the economy.
This has caused serious/great damage to the economy.

19) I still remember <u>those thoughtless days playing with the other children</u>.
I still remember those carefree days playing with the other children.
"Thoughtless" has a negative connotation: a "thoughtless person" acts without consideration for others; his/her actions may also be described as "thoughtless". "Carefree" has a positive connotation: it gives the idea of an absence of worries.

20) It is difficult to <u>reconquer my trust</u>.

It is difficult to win back/regain my trust.

"Reconquer" is less versatile than the Italian "riconquistare" and is generally used only in military contexts.

21) I developed <u>a big passion</u> for the cinema.

I developed a great passion for the cinema.

22) The salary is not enough <u>to rear a family</u>.

The salary is not enough to raise a family.

"Rear" is generally used for livestock ("He abandoned his career as a banker and retired to the country to rear pigs"), "raise" for human beings ("Raising children is never an easy task").

23) The <u>sea level will arise</u>.

The sea level will rise.

Problems arise, levels rise (and fall).

24) Unfortunately <u>his family had economic problems</u>.

Unfortunately his family had financial problems.

"Economic" means "relating to the economy" ("economic growth"; "economic policy"; "economic crisis"; etc); We usually use the expression "economic problems" when talking about a country or a geographical area (e.g. "Like much of Europe, southern Italy has serious economic problems").

25) It was <u>a school managed by sisters</u>.

It was a school run by nuns.

"Managed" is mostly used to translate "gestire" in the context of a business while with non-commercial organisations the more usual term is "run". "Sister" is used to translate "suora" as part of a name ("Sister Mary") or as a term of address ("Good morning, Sister").

26) She is working as <u>an apprentice in a lawyer's office</u>.

She is working as a trainee / an articled clerk in a lawyer's office.

The term "apprentice" is generally used with reference to manual work ("He is working as an apprentice mechanic"). "Trainee" may be used for most kinds of work; "articled clerk" is specific to the legal profession. See also 5) in the chapter False Friends.

27) I <u>frequented elementary school</u> in Rome.

I went to elementary/primary school in Rome.

"To frequent" is much less common than the Italian "frequentare". It is primarily used in the context of leisure activities ("she used to frequent that bar"; "it's not the kind of restaurant they frequent"). Note that although "elementary school" is the preferred term in the USA, speakers in the UK use "primary school".

28) It's a good way to <u>expand your personal dictionary</u>.

It's a good way to expand your personal vocabulary.

Use "dictionary" when referring to the book, "vocabulary" as a synonym for words in general or for the words somebody knows.

29) <u>I soon understood that</u> I was wrong.

I soon realised that I was wrong.

When translating "capire" in the sense of "rendersi conto", it is more usual to use the verb "realise".

30) I always <u>weight the ingredients</u> carefully.

I always weigh the ingredients carefully.

To translate "pesare", use "weigh" when the sense – as in this example – is "determine the weight of", and "weight" when the sense is "apply a coefficient to" – as in statistical analyses.

31) The problem has been caused by <u>strong industrial development</u>.

The problem has been caused by extensive industrial development.

EXERCISES

A. Choose the more appropriate of the two alternatives:

1) We were introduced by a *mutual/common* friend.

2) Estate agents *earn/gain* a lot more money than teachers.

3) At the beginning of the 20th century, Maria Montessori introduced a new educational *way/approach*.

4) What kind of results do you hope to *achieve/reach*?

5) We *lived/had* some great times together.

6) It's a beautiful building but it needs *renovating/restructuring*.

7) She has a *big/great* passion for art.

8) What kind of school did you *frequent/go to*?

9) Because of his *financial/economic* problems, my brother has had to take on a second job.

10) I prefer films with happy *endings/finals*.

11) Learning a foreign language is an excellent way to *expand/broaden* your cultural *horizons/baggage*.

12) We had a wonderful, *thoughtless/carefree* childhood.

B. Write answers to the following questions, then ask the questions to your study partner and make a note of his/her answers:

1) Where did you go to primary school?

2) Has your house been renovated recently?

3) Do you always weigh the ingredients when you cook?

4) Can you remember the ending of a book or film that really surprised you?

5) What is your greatest passion?

6) What are the best ways to broaden your cultural horizons?

7) How do you go about expanding your English vocabulary?

Comparatives & Superlatives

1) It's <u>more near</u>.
It's nearer.

2) George is younger <u>of</u> his brother.
George is younger than his brother.

3) Now I'm stronger <u>that</u> before.
Now I'm stronger than before.

4) I would like to do something <u>funnier</u>, like shopping!
I would like to do something more fun, like shopping!
Distinguish "funnier", meaning something that makes you laugh more, from "more fun", which means "more enjoyable". See also 18) and 19) in the chapter Adjectives.

5) It offers <u>less</u> job opportunities.
It offers fewer job opportunities.
This is a mistake that many native speakers also make. Use "less" with uncountable nouns ("less water"; "less money"; etc), "fewer" with countable nouns.

6) I felt my English was getting <u>worst</u>.
I felt my English was getting worse.
Note that "to get worse" has an antonym: "to get better".

7) I grew up in the same village <u>of</u> my boyfriend.
I grew up in the same village as my boyfriend.

8) I'm sure if I had done the oral part <u>in a better way</u>, I would have passed the exam.
I'm sure if I had done the oral part better, I would have passed the exam.

9) <u>Is not so important a happy ending than</u> a realistic plot.
A happy ending is not as important as a realistic plot.

10) Everyone tries to do his <u>better</u>.
Everyone tries to do his best.

11) It's the thing I <u>more</u> dislike.
It's the thing I most dislike.

12) I decided to see if my dog was my <u>faithfullest</u> friend.

I decided to see if my dog was my most faithful friend.

Use "more", not "-er", and "most", not -est", to make the comparative and superlative forms of any adjective ending in "-ful" ("more useful", "most useful").

13) I spend <u>the most part of</u> my time studying.

I spend most of my time studying.

The phrase "the most part" is rarely used except in the expression "for the most part" ("There is some administrative work but for the most part the job involves dealing with the public"). See also 14) and 15) below.

14) I would spend <u>the most part of</u> my money on useful things.

I would spend most of my money on useful things.

15) Most <u>of</u> works in the existing literature do not take account of this.

Most works in the existing literature do not take account of this.

16) There should be at <u>less</u> four bedrooms.

There should be at least four bedrooms.

17) What is the <u>most</u> hardest thing to do?

What is the hardest thing to do?

18) I've always been the smallest <u>of</u> the class.

I've always been the smallest in the class.

19) The town is in the <u>southest</u> part of the region.

The town is in the southernmost part of the region.

EXERCISES

A. Match each sentence beginning to a suitable ending:

1) Which of the two holidays...

2) We'll need at...

3) My cold is getting...

4) Out of all these problems, unemployment is the...

5) There was less...

6) Money is not as...

7) Which of the two jokes...

8) It is more...

9) There were fewer...

10) These days he spends...

11) The problem is the same...

12) It is much...

a) ...traffic than I expected.

b) ...people than last time.

c) ...was more fun?

d) ...as before.

e) ...useful than you might think.

f) ...nearer than the other supermarket.

g) ...most of his time gardening.

h) ...worst.

i) ...least another five hundred grams.

j) ...did you think was funnier?

k) ...worse and worse.

l) ...important as some people seem to believe.

B. Correct each sentence by changing one word:

1) It is more interesting that the other one.

2) Just try to do your better.

3) Where in the world would you more like to live?

4) It will cost at less €50.

5) Who is the brightest student of the class?

6) Mine is the same of yours.

7) Lecce is not as big than Naples.

8) They live in the northest part of Scotland.

C. Write answers to the following questions, then ask the questions to your study partner and make a note of his/her answers:

1) What are the things you consider more fun than shopping?

2) Do you live nearer to the mountains or the sea?

3) Is your English getting better or worse?

4) What is the thing you most dislike?

5) What is the hardest thing about English?

6) In your opinion, what is the most interesting town in your region?

7) What do you spend most of your money on?

Conjunctions

1) I will succeed <u>because of</u> I'm determined.

I will succeed because I'm determined.

Use "because of" before a noun, pronoun or noun phrase ("because of the rain"; "because of him"; "because of the way she behaved"); use "because" before a verb phrase.

2) She is studying English <u>why</u> she wants to live in London.

She is studying English because she wants to live in London.

Compare "She is studying English, which is why she wants to live in London".

3) I can't decide between the cheesecake <u>or</u> the mousse.

I can't decide between the cheesecake and the mousse.

4) You can stay here <u>until</u> you like.

You can stay here as long as you like.

Distinguish "until" ("finché non") from "as long as" (finché). See also 5) below.

5) I plan to continue working <u>until</u> I have the energy.

I plan to continue working as long as I have the energy.

6) <u>In case</u> you see her, say "Happy Birthday" from me.

If you see her, say "Happy Birthday" from me.

Compare "Say 'Happy Birthday' from me in case I don't get to see her myself".

7) She will not understand <u>unless</u> you don't explain.

She will not understand unless you explain.

"Unless" is usually translated as "a meno che non": to avoid mistakes like the one in this example, it may be useful to think of the "un-" prefix as the equivalent of the Italian "non". Note that in this case the intended sense could also be conveyed by "She will not understand if you don't explain".

8) I don't know <u>if</u> to accept.

I don't know whether to accept.

Use "whether" in preference to "if" when translating "se" (in the sense of "se...oppure no") before an infinitive.

9) He bought a new computer yesterday <u>even if</u> he already has a good one.

He bought a new computer yesterday even though he already has a good one.

Use "even though" in preference to "even if" when referring to a real rather than hypothetical situation.

10) She continued to work <u>in spite of</u> she was expecting her first child.

She continued to work in spite of the fact [that] she was expecting her first child. / She continued to work although she was expecting her first child. / She continued to work even though she was expecting her first child.

11) I love the theatre, <u>instead</u> my boyfriend prefers the cinema.

I love the theatre while my boyfriend prefers the cinema. / I love the theatre. My boyfriend, on the other hand, prefers the cinema.

EXERCISES

A. Insert an appropriate conjunction into each sentence (one letter per space):

1) He quit his job _ _ _ _ _ _ _ he couldn't live on such a low salary.

2) I'll take my credit card _ _ _ _ _ _ they don't accept cash.

3) _ _ _ _ _ _ _ _ _ the sea was quite rough, there were people swimming off the local beach.

4) For their honeymoon they are undecided between Japan _ _ _ New Zealand.

5) Their electricity will be cut off _ _ _ _ _ _ they pay the bill by tomorrow.

6) We can't decide _ _ _ _ _ _ _ to go or not.

7) She doesn't speak the language _ _ _ _ _ _ _ _ _ _ she has been living there for years.

8) They wouldn't be able to afford that house _ _ _ _ _ _ they won the lottery.

9) I'll love you _ _ _ _ _ I die and I hope you'll love me _ _ _ _ _ _ _ _ you live!

10) Those on the left are pushing for better services _ _ _ _ _ those on the right want lower taxes.

11) He just went ahead and did it _ _ _ _ _ _ _ _ _ _ _ _ _ _ _ _ I had warned him not to.

B. Write answers to the following questions, then ask the questions to your study partner and make a note of his/her answers:

1) How do you decide whether to have a dessert or not?

2) Are there any foods you eat for health reasons even though you don't like them?

3) Would you accept the offer of your ideal job even if it meant moving abroad?

4) How effectively can you study while you are listening to music?

5) What are the experiences you will remember as long as you live?

Countable and Uncountable Nouns

1) I'm trying to find a work.

I'm trying to find work. / I'm trying to find a job.

"Work" in the sense of "lavoro" is uncountable. As a countable noun it means "opera" (e.g. "a work of art"; "the works of Shakespeare"). Note also "The motorway is closed because of road works".

2) A video is better than a photography.

A video is better than a photograph.

"Photography" is uncountable: it refers to the art or the activity, not to a single image.

3) He wrote a poetry about the sea.

He wrote a poem about the sea.

"Poetry" is uncountable ("He is an expert on romantic poetry").

4) It was a very long travel.

It was a very long trip/journey.

Although it is occasionally used in the plural ("What did you see on your travels?"), "travel" is an uncountable noun (e.g. "I like travel"). "Journey" refers to travel between two points ("The journey from Milan to Rome took them five hours"). "Trip" usually includes the journey(s) and the time spent at the destination ("How was your trip to London last month?"). See also 2) in the chapter Classics.

5) It has many seasides with black sand.

It has many beaches with black sand.

"Seaside" is uncountable and is usually generic rather than specific ("In the summer we take the children to the seaside as often as we can").

6) These informations are useful.

This information is useful.

"Information" is uncountable.

7) He takes care of the serious stuffs.

He takes care of the serious stuff.

"Stuff" is uncountable.

8) I love to feel the wind <u>between my hairs</u>.

I love to feel the wind in my hair.

The countable noun "hairs" means "peli". "Capelli" is translated with the uncountable noun "hair".

9) On Saturday mornings I usually try to do all the <u>houseworks</u>.

On Saturday mornings I usually try to do all the housework.

Like "homework" ("compiti a casa"), "housework" ("servizi") is uncountable.

10) I didn't have as <u>many</u> time as I would have liked.

I didn't have as much time as I would have liked.

Distinguish "as many times as" ("tante volte quante") from "as much time as" ("tanto tempo quanto").

11) There is <u>a</u> rich vegetation.

There is rich vegetation. / The vegetation is rich.

12) <u>Advices</u> are welcome.

Advice is welcome.

13) The earthquake caused a lot of <u>damages</u>.

The earthquake caused a lot of damage.

"Damages" is generally only used to mean the compensation awarded by a court to a person or organisation that has been damaged (not necessarily physically) in some way.

14) <u>Researches</u> show that the problem is getting worse.

Research shows that the problem is getting worse.

15) The <u>number</u> of industrial waste has increased.

The amount of industrial waste has increased.

EXERCISES

A. Choose the more appropriate of the two alternatives:

1) This one is definitely my favourite Neruda *poetry/poem*.

2) Do you prefer prose or *poetry/poem*?

3) She's extremely interested in *photography/photograph*.

4) I love that *photography/photograph* of you holding the baby.
5) We have a lot of *work/job* to do today.
6) My friend Margherita has found a *work/job* with a company in Sweden.
7) How was your *trip/travel* to San Francisco?
8) They say that *trip/travel* broadens the mind.
9) How far is it to the nearest *seaside/beach*?
10) I'm going to have my *hair/hairs* cut this afternoon.

B. Write answers to the following questions, then ask the questions to your study partner and make a note of his/her answers:
1) Have you ever had a job?
2) When did you last have your hair cut?
3) Is there a beach near where you live?
4) Have you ever written a poem?
5) How long is your journey to school/university/work?
6) Do you devote more time to your homework or to the housework?
7) If you could only keep one photograph, which one would it be?
8) Who are the people you most often ask for advice?
9) Are you spending as much time as you should studying English?

Definite Article

OMISSION OF ARTICLE WHERE REQUIRED

1) After I was born, my parents decided to live <u>in country</u>.
After I was born, my parents decided to live in the country.

2) We went <u>to swimming pool</u> twice a week.
We went to the swimming pool twice a week.

3) I like to go <u>in mountain</u> in the summer.
I like to go to the mountains in the summer.

4) My grandmother lives <u>in mountain</u>.
My grandmother lives in the mountains.

5) You left it <u>in kitchen</u>.
You left it in the kitchen.
Compare 16) in the chapter Indefinite Article.

6) My father works <u>in navy</u>.
My father works in the navy.

7) He met her <u>on train</u>.
He met her on the train.

INCLUSION OF ARTICLE WHERE NOT REQUIRED

8) In <u>the</u> recent years I have done several jobs.
In recent years I have done several jobs.

9) I played basketball at <u>the</u> primary school.
I played basketball at primary school.
Compare: "Next week there is a basketball tournament at the primary school opposite the park."

10) He has just finished <u>the</u> college.
He has just finished college.

11) After <u>the</u> secondary school I never saw him again.
After secondary school I never saw him again.

12) I started <u>the</u> university in <u>the</u> 2010.
I started university in 2010.

13) I like <u>the</u> school and <u>the study</u>.
I like school and studying. / I like the school and studying.
Distinguish "I like the school" (referring to a specific institution) from "I like school" (referring to the educational experience).

14) We recycle <u>the</u> 70% of our household waste.
We recycle 70% of our household waste.

15) I played with <u>the</u> dolls or I watched <u>the</u> cartoons.
I played with dolls or I watched cartoons.
Use of "the" is only appropriate if the interlocutor knows exactly which dolls and cartoons the speaker is referring to.

16) At the moment <u>the</u> life couldn't be better.
At the moment life couldn't be better.

17) We are all equal in <u>the</u> life.
We are all equal in life.

18) It is set in <u>the</u> fourth century Alexandria.
It is set in fourth century Alexandria.

19) She saw <u>the</u> Noah's picture in the newspaper.
She saw Noah's picture in the newspaper.

20) She was a fan of <u>the</u> Manchester United.
She was a fan of Manchester United. / She was a Manchester United fan.

21) I started travelling alone all over <u>the</u> Europe.
I started travelling alone all over Europe.

22) It started <u>the</u> last week and finishes <u>the</u> next week.
It started last week and finishes next week.

23) <u>In the</u> last September I started an English course.
Last September I started an English course.

24) In ~~the~~ February 2011 I finally graduated.
In February 2011 I finally graduated.

25) ~~The~~ good wins over ~~the~~ evil.
Good wins over evil.

26) ~~The~~ English is a much more difficult language than ~~the~~ German.
English is a much more difficult language than German.
Distinguish "the English" and "the Germans" (the peoples) from "English" and "German" (the languages).

27) More and more tourists are visiting ~~the~~ southern Italy.
More and more tourists are visiting southern Italy.

28) We went with the plane.
We went by plane.

OTHER
29) In Puglia there is a very beautiful sea.
The sea in Puglia is very beautiful.

EXERCISES

A. For each gap, decide whether or not to insert "the":

1) We often go walking in _____ countryside or in _____ mountains.

2) My brother supports _____ Juventus but I support _____ Inter.

3) Mum's cooking in _____ kitchen and Dad's working in _____ garden.

4) They came by _____ bus but they're going back on _____ train.

5) In _____ recent years he has been working less.

6) I loved _____ primary school, hated _____ secondary school and quite like _____ university.

7) I read somewhere that _____ 55% of children in _____ Europe watch _____ cartoons every day.

8) Vandals set fire to _____ secondary school opposite our house _____ last week.

9) I imagine that _____ life in _____ 16th century London was very different from today.

10) _____ Lucy's picture was in _____ newspaper _____ last month.

43

B. Write answers to the following questions, then ask the questions to your study partner and make a note of his/her answers:

1) How's life at the moment?

2) Do you prefer the mountains or the sea?

3) How old were you in 2013?

4) Do you spend more time in the kitchen or in the bathroom?

5) How many countries in Europe have you been to?

6)) What languages do you speak?

7) Did you prefer primary school or secondary school?

8) What percentage of your time do you spend studying?

9) How hard have you been working in recent weeks?

Different Language, Different Structure

1) If I read a new book and <u>it doesn't like me</u>, I don't finish reading it.
If I read a new book and I don't like it, I don't finish reading it.
See also 37) in the chapter Word Order.

2) <u>It is easy that</u> people like it.
People tend to like it.

3) I would have preferred to attend a singing course but my parents <u>didn't want it</u>.
I would have preferred to attend a singing course but my parents didn't want me to.
"It" is used to refer back to a noun ("I offered him my seat but he didn't want it"), not to a verb.

4) This film <u>opens eyes to people</u>.
This film opens people's eyes.

5) <u>I wish me</u> a peaceful life.
I hope to have a peaceful life.

6) I spent <u>the summer of my ten years</u> waiting for a letter from Hogwarts.
When I was ten, I spent the summer waiting for a letter from Hogwarts. / As a ten-year-old, I spent the summer waiting for a letter from Hogwarts.

7) <u>It's for that</u> I'll always love her.
That's [the reason] why I'll always love her.

8) <u>Here you are my essay</u>.
Here is my essay. / Here you are.
"Here you are!" is a stand-alone phrase used when you hand or send your interlocutor what he/she has requested or is expecting.

9) When there isn't an interesting film <u>in programme</u>, I spend the evening in a pub.
When there isn't an interesting film on, I spend the evening in a pub.

10) I <u>have a bit of fear</u>.
I am a little afraid.

11) In front of me <u>there is decisively a crossroads</u>!
I am definitely at a crossroads in my life!

12) Your concentration must always be <u>at maximum</u>.
Your concentration levels must always be as high as possible.

13) I passed <u>the exams for a driver's licence</u>.
I passed my driving test.

14) <u>By this time</u>, shopping after an exam is a habit.
It has got to the point where shopping after an exam has become a habit.

15) <u>In the last period of my life</u> I graduated from high school.
I [have] recently finished secondary school. (UK) / I recently graduated from high school. (US)

16) It <u>left me without breath</u>.
It took my breath away.

17) He has lost <u>the only reason of his life</u>.
He has lost the only thing he had to live for.

18) <u>He feels to be</u> different from other people.
He feels different from other people. / He feels he is different from other people.

19) These are characteristics <u>I feel to have</u>.
These are characteristics I feel I have.

20) <u>You can give no answer</u>.
You don't have to answer.

21) <u>I'm looking for someone who looks after my daughter</u> in the afternoons.
I'm looking for someone to look after my daughter in the afternoons.

22) <u>I don't know if it's better that you</u> give me the original or the translated version.
I don't know if it's better for you to give me the original or the translated version.

23) We have similar tastes and <u>a similar way of conceiving the couple</u>.
We have similar tastes and a similar idea of what it means to be a couple.

24) She <u>risks to get back to the beginning</u>.
She risks finding herself back at square one.

25) One of them is <u>called as my father</u>.
One of them has the same name as my father.

26) I've always been <u>a good fork</u>.
I've always been a good eater. / I've always liked my food.

27) When I meet new people, <u>I don't give a good impression of me</u>.
When I meet new people, I don't make a good impression.

28) I would like to <u>leave a good memory of me</u>.
I would like to be well remembered. / I would like people to have good memories of me.

29) <u>I made an investment, buying</u> an ipad.
I made an investment and bought an ipad.

30) I go to a dance school <u>in my city, Gravina</u>.
I go to a dance school in Gravina, the town where I live.
In English, the term "city" is reserved for places of great size, population or importance. As a rule of thumb, if an Italian "città" is not a "capoluogo", it is more likely to be a "town" than a "city".

31) I looked on the table but <u>there isn't</u>.
I looked on the table but it isn't there.

EXERCISES

A. In each sentence, replace the underlined phrase with one taken from the list below:
1) <u>It's for that</u> she will never do it.
2) Are there any good films <u>in programme</u> this week?
3) Your concentration must always be <u>at maximum</u>.
4) He passed <u>the exams for a driver's licence</u>.
5) <u>By this time,</u> I don't believe anything Italian politicians say.
6) <u>In the last period of my life I have</u> started a yoga course.

7) He has lost the only <u>reason of his life</u>.

8) You <u>can give no</u> answer.

9) We have similar tastes and a similar <u>way of conceiving the</u> couple.

10) You risk <u>to get back to the beginning</u>.

11) One of them <u>is called as</u> my father.

12) I would like to <u>leave a good memory of me</u>.

a) be well remembered

b) as great as possible

c) don't have to

d) finding yourself back at square one.

e) has the same name as

f) that's [the reason] why

g) his driving test.

h) I have recently

i) it has got to the point where

j) on

k) idea of what it means to be a

l) thing he had to live for

B. Write answers to the following questions, then ask the questions to your study partner and make a note of his/her answers:

1) Are there any good films on near you this week?

2) Can you give an example of something that took your breath away?

3) In what ways do you feel you are different from other people?

4) Have you passed your driving test yet?

5) Do you tend to get angry easily?

6) Have you done anything recently that your family didn't want you to?

7) Is there anyone you know that you are a little afraid of?

Do & Make

USING "DO" WHERE "MAKE" IS REQUIRED
1) I've <u>done</u> a lot of mistakes.
I've made a lot of mistakes.

2) At the age of eight I <u>did</u> my first creation.
At the age of eight I made my first creation.

3) I would like to <u>do</u> some changes in my house.
I would like to make some changes in my house.

4) My parents work hard and <u>do</u> a lot of sacrifices.
My parents work hard and make a lot of sacrifices.

5) I have <u>done</u> a little investment.
I have made a little investment.

6) Politicians should <u>do</u> a special effort to solve this problem.
Politicians should make a special effort to solve this problem.

7) Since the 18th century, man has done a lot of progress in the scientific field.
Since the 18th century, man has made a lot of progress in the scientific field.

USING "MAKE" WHERE "DO" IS REQUIRED
8) I wish to go around the world making literary research.
I wish to go around the world doing literary research.

9) At primary school I always <u>made</u> my homework.
At primary school I always did my homework.

10) At the moment I'm <u>making</u> repetitions to a 14-year-old boy.
At the moment I'm doing private lessons with a 14-year-old boy.

USING "DO" WHERE ANOTHER VERB IS REQUIRED
11) It was the worst experience that I've ever <u>done</u>.
It was the worst experience that I've ever had.

12) I would like to <u>do</u> the journalist.

I would like to be a journalist.

13) On Saturday afternoons I <u>do</u> shopping with my boyfriend.

On Saturday afternoons I go shopping with my boyfriend.

Distinguish "go shopping" ("fare shopping") from "do the shopping" ("fare la spesa").

14) I hope you are well and have <u>done</u> a nice holiday!

I hope you are well and have had a nice holiday!

15) When I get home I need to <u>do</u> a shower.

When I get home I need to have/take a shower.

16) The first action to <u>do</u> is to make people more aware.

The first action to take is to make people more aware.

USING ANOTHER VERB WHERE "DO" IS REQUIRED

17) I don't <u>practise</u> any sports; I prefer to read or listen to music.

I don't do/play any sports; I prefer to read or listen to music.

18) This month I'm going to <u>give</u> my second exam.

This month I'm going to do/take my second exam.

USING "MAKE" WHERE ANOTHER VERB IS REQUIRED

19) I like to <u>make</u> photos.

I like to take photos.

20) He <u>makes</u> various feats.

He performs various feats.

21) She <u>makes</u> a simple action.

She performs a simple action.

22) Human beings have <u>made</u> a lot of damage to the environment.

Human beings have caused a lot of damage to the environment.

23) It has a small harbour where we <u>make</u> our walks.
It has a small harbour where we go for walks. / It has a small harbour where we take [our] walks.

24) For the occasion I <u>made</u> a huge party.
For the occasion I had/threw a huge party.

25) I hope to <u>make me a family</u> with Domenico.
I hope to have a family with Domenico.

26) This friendship <u>made us grow</u>.
This friendship helped us to grow.

27) I would like to <u>make</u> this experience again.
I would like to repeat this experience.

28) I hoped to <u>make</u> you check my exercises but you were very busy.
I hoped to get you to check my exercises but you were very busy.
"To make someone do something" means to force them to do it ("Her mum makes her go to church every Sunday").

29) Her presence <u>made</u> me distract.
Her presence distracted me.

30) The bishop decides to <u>make</u> kill the woman.
The bishop decides to have the woman killed.

31) Factories keep on <u>making</u> waste and discharging it into rivers.
Factories keep on producing waste and discharging it into rivers.

USING ANOTHER VERB WHERE "MAKE" IS REQUIRED
32) I also like to <u>prepare</u> cakes.
I also like to make cakes.

33) A teacher <u>imposed</u> me to read a page of my diary in front of all the class.
A teacher made me read a page of my diary in front of all the class.

EXERCISES

A. Complete the sentences by inserting a suitable form of "do" or "make":

1) She _____ a serious mistake in marrying him.

2) Have you _____ your homework yet?

3) I can't find a job but I'm _____ private lessons with some schoolchildren.

4) You need to _____ some changes to this before you submit it.

5) I have had to _____ a lot of sacrifices to be able to continue my studies.

6) It took three years to _____ the necessary research for this project.

7) I'll _____ you a cake for your birthday if you like.

8) When are you _____ your next exam?

9) Did you _____ any sports when you were at school?

10) I didn't want to but the teacher _____ me rewrite it.

B. Correct the sentences by replacing "do" or "make" with a verb from the list provided:

be   get   go for   go   had   have (2)   helped   perform   repeat   take

1) My wife likes to <u>do</u> shopping with my credit card.

2) I've never <u>done</u> such a bad experience.

3) When she grows up she wants to <u>do</u> an engineer.

4) Did you <u>do</u> a nice holiday?

5) Could you <u>make</u> a photo of us, please?

6) I think I might <u>make</u> a walk along the seafront.

7) They decided to <u>make</u> a really big party to celebrate their engagement.

8) Changing my diet <u>made</u> me get better.

9) We would like to <u>make again</u> this experience.

10) He was able to <u>make</u> some remarkable feats.

11) Can't you <u>make</u> your boss to buy you a new computer?

C. Write answers to the following questions, then ask the questions to your study partner and make a note of his/her answers:

1) What changes would you like to make in your house?

2) Who does the shopping in your family?

3) How often do you go shopping for clothes?

4) What's the worst culinary experience you have ever had?

5) When did you last have a party?

6) Do you prefer to take photos with a phone or a traditional camera?
7) What kind of mistakes do you make most frequently in English?
8) How much progress have you made in English since last year?

False Friends

1) I put it on the top shelf of my <u>library</u>.

I put it on the top shelf of my bookcase.

"Library" means biblioteca"; "libreria" is "bookshop" or, in the case of the piece of furniture, "bookcase".

2) The holiday was a big <u>delusion</u>.

The holiday was a big disappointment.

A "delusion" is a form of "illusion" ("He suffers from delusions of grandeur").

3) She is a <u>very</u> genius.

She is a real genius. / She is a true genius.

Although "very" is occasionally found before nouns ("a very picture of loveliness"), the best strategy for language students is to use it only with adjectives and adverbs. See also 4) below.

4) Singing is my <u>very</u> passion.

Singing is my real passion. / Singing is my true passion.

5) Next summer I will start a <u>stage</u> in Milan.

Next summer I will start a training course / an internship / an apprenticeship / on-the-job training in Milan.

"Training course" and "on-the-job training" are generic; use "apprenticeship" for manual-type jobs and "internship" for training for a professional career. See also 26) in the chapter Collocations.

6) I started attending <u>lyrical</u> singing lessons.

I started attending opera-singing lessons.

The adjective "lyrical" means "beautifully artistic" or "expressive of emotion" ("a lyrical account of her childhood"; "one of the more lyrical passages in the novel").

7) I love to <u>pass</u> time with all my friends.

I love to spend time with all my friends.

The expression "pass the time" (note that in this case we add "the") is generally used to give the idea that we want that time to go quickly ("I walked round the duty-free shops to pass the time while I was waiting for my flight").

8) We didn't have the <u>possibility</u> to do it.

We didn't have the chance/opportunity to do it.

9) I was brought up in a <u>factory</u> with a lot of animals.

I was brought up on a farm with a lot of animals.

A "factory" is where goods are manufactured on an industrial scale.

10) "Dead Poets Society" is the story of an English <u>professor</u>.

"Dead Poets Society" is the story of an English teacher.

A "professor" is a high-level university teacher.

11) It was directed by the <u>genial</u> Quentin Tarantino.

It was directed by the brilliant Quentin Tarantino.

"Genial" means "amichevole" or "cordiale".

12) I got excellent <u>votes</u> in all the exams.

I got excellent marks in all the exams.

"Votes" are what people cast in elections.

13) I lived in an <u>ancient</u> <u>condominium</u>.

I lived in an old apartment building.

It is more usual to translate "anziano" with "old" than "ancient", which usually corresponds to "antico" ("This was a common practice in ancient Greece") or is used for extreme emphasis ("Her great-grandmother is positively ancient").
"Condominium" is rarely used in British English but is common, especially in the abbreviated form "condo", in the US and Canada.

14) My father worked as a <u>geometer</u>.

My father worked as a surveyor.

The word "geometer" means "expert in geometry". It is rarely used.

15) At the age of 16, I won a <u>premium</u> of €1,000 in a <u>scientific concourse</u>.

At the age of 16, I won a prize of €1,000 in a science competition.

Depending on the context, "concorso" can also be translated as "competitive exam", "open competition" or "invitation to tender".

16) I still <u>preserve</u> two friends from middle school.

I still have two friends from middle school.

"Preserve" is generally used for food products ("She preserves the peppers in oil"); it

can be used figuratively but is best avoided when you are referring to living things you don't intend to eat or exhibit.

17) I don't know if I will marry my <u>actual</u> boyfriend.

I don't know if I will marry my current boyfriend.

"Actual" means "vero", "reale" or "vero e proprio" ("I have no problem with the practice tests but I'm still worried about the actual exam").

18) If I won the lottery, I would help my father to start up a new <u>activity</u>.

If I won the lottery, I would help my father to start up a new business.

19) He <u>exposes</u> his own ideas about this.

He explains his own ideas about this.

The verb "to expose" is most frequently used in the sense of "to bring to light" something hidden, such as corrupt or criminal activity ("The bank's illegal dealings were exposed by a British newspaper").

20) I <u>pretend</u> the same things from other people.

I expect the same things from other people.

The English verb "pretend" means "fingere" ("She pretended not to see him").

21) I like reading Stephen King's <u>romances</u>.

I like reading Stephen King's novels.

A "romance" is a sentimental book with love as its main theme.

22) A lot of my <u>parents</u> live in Sicily.

A lot of my relatives live in Sicily.

Your "parents" are your mother and father, and nobody else.

23) The film was so <u>annoying</u> that I fell asleep.

The film was so boring that I fell asleep.

"Annoying" means "irritating".

24) I had a <u>toast</u> for lunch.

I had a toasted [ham and cheese] sandwich for lunch.

The English word "toast" is uncountable and means simply "pane tostato" ("He usually just has toast and marmalade for breakfast").

25) The receptionist was very <u>gentle</u> with us.

The receptionist was very kind to us.

The word "gentle" – especially when followed by "with" – is most frequently used to suggest a delicate physical touch ("You can hold the baby but you must be gentle with him"). It is not used in contemporary English as a synonym of "polite" or "courteous".

26) My father is an <u>advocate</u> and he works in a law firm in Molfetta.

My father is a lawyer and he works in a law firm in Molfetta.

Although the word "advocate" is occasionally used to refer to a very specific type of lawyer, it is more usually employed in the sense of "proponent" or "supporter" ("He is a strong advocate of the legalisation of drugs").

27) Italian Literature is my favourite <u>matter</u>.

Italian Literature is my favourite subject.

The term "matter" can be synonymous with "subject" in its broader sense of "question" or "issue" ("They are meeting tomorrow to discuss the matter") but is not used to denote a specific field of study.

28) He died in an <u>incident</u>.

He died in an accident.

"Incident" is a generic term for an event or an occurrence ("I can remember several amusing incidents from that holiday"); an "accident" is a specific type of incident usually involving some kind of injury or damage ("He hurt his leg in a car accident").

29) She is always <u>nervous</u> when she is tired and hungry.

She is always irritable when she is tired and hungry.

"Nervous" describes the feeling of agitation or apprehension you might experience before an exam, a first date or a visit to the dentist.

30) The problem of pollution <u>touches</u> us all.

The problem of pollution affects us all.

If something "touches" us (in a non-physical sense), it moves us emotionally.

31) I live in a modern <u>palace</u> in Cerignola.

I live in a modern apartment building/block in Cerignola.

EXERCISES

A. Correct the sentences by replacing the underlined error with a noun from the list provided:

accident   bookcase   business   disappointment   farm   marks
novel   opportunity   relatives   subject   teacher   training course

1) We have so many books we had to buy a new <u>library</u>.

2) She is currently doing a <u>stage</u> in Milan.

3) Not passing the exam was an enormous <u>delusion</u>.

4) I hope to have the <u>possibility</u> to travel abroad.

5) We buy our fruit and vegetables from a local <u>factory</u>.

6) My sister is a <u>professor</u> in a secondary school.

7) I studied economics and my dream is to start my own <u>activity</u>.

8) His latest <u>romance</u> is about the Vietnam War.

9) I spent Christmas Day with about twenty of my <u>parents</u>.

10) My <u>votes</u> in maths were never good.

11) I like school; history is the only <u>matter</u> I don't enjoy.

12) The road was blocked because of a bad car <u>incident</u>.

B. Underline the most appropriate adjective in each sentence:

1) This painting is a *very / real / truly* masterpiece.

2) For many *lyrical / melodrama / opera* singers, performing at La Scala will only ever be a dream.

3) She never has anything interesting to say: I get *bored / annoyed / asleep* just thinking about her!

4) You have to read it: it's *genial / congenial / brilliant*!

5) The *current / actual / topical* economic crisis is much worse than the last one.

6) My colleague will now *expose / explain / exhibit* in more detail how the device works.

7) The only people left in the village now are *ancient / old / antique* or middle-aged.

8) Thank you so much! It's really *gentle / delicate / kind* of you!

9) He is often *nervous / sinewy / irritable* when he has had a hard day at work.

C. Write answers to the following questions, then ask the questions to your study partner and make a note of his/her answers:

1) Would you prefer to work in a library or in a bookshop?

2) Which subjects did you get your highest marks in at school?

3) Would you rather own a factory or a farm?

4) When do you get nervous?

5) What makes you irritable?

6) Have you ever won a prize?

7) What are the disadvantages of living in an apartment building?

8) What was the last novel you read?

9) Have you had any disappointments recently?

Impersonal "it"

OMISSION OF "IT"

1) I take 25 minutes to get to university.

It takes [me] 25 minutes to get to university.

2) In Italy is traditional to be named after one's grandparents.

In Italy it is traditional to be named after one's grandparents.

3) Is important to remember this.

It is important to remember this.

The structure "it + verb 'to be' + adjective [+ not] + to infinitive" is very common ("it is useful to know"; "it will be difficult to convince her"; "it was wrong not to tell him"; etc) but – as can be seen in 5) below – it is not used with all adjectives.

4) Who is?

Who is it?

Note that "it" is also used in the response ("It's me"; "It's your sister"; It's us"; etc). See also 1) in the chapter Questions.

MISUSE OF "IT"

5) It is urgent to change our eating habits.

We urgently need to change our eating habits. / There is an urgent need for us to change our eating habits.

6) It's very good their relationship .

It's a very good relationship they have. / Their relationship is very good.

7) Sometimes it's enough a walk in the rain.

Sometimes a walk in the rain is enough.

8) Taking the bus or the train it's better than using the car.

Taking the bus or the train is better than using the car. / It's better to take the train or bus than to use the car.

9) It should never be forgotten what happened.

What happened should never be forgotten.

10) I realize that it is necessary a lot of courage.
I realize that a lot of courage is necessary.

11) I think about how much time it has passed.
I think about how much time has passed.

12) Perhaps it would have been some hope.
Perhaps there would have been some hope.

EXERCISE

Write answers to the following questions, then ask the questions to your study partner and make a note of his/her answers:
1) How long does it take you to get dressed in the morning?
2) What are the things in life that it is most important to remember?
3) In your family what is it traditional to eat at Christmas?
4) How would you describe your relationship with your neighbours?
5) Which is more difficult: listening to English or speaking English?

Indefinite Article

"A" OR "AN"

1) She is <u>an</u> housewife.

She is a housewife.

"A" becomes "an" before initial "h" only in those rare cases where the "h" is not pronounced (e.g. "an hour"; "an honour"; "an heir"; "an honest man"; "an honourable defeat"; etc). See also 2) and 3) below.

2) They bought <u>an</u> house in Bitritto.

They bought a house in Bitritto.

3) My mother used to work as <u>an</u> hairdresser.

My mother used to work as a hairdresser.

4) He is <u>an</u> university professor.

He is a university professor.

In a number of words beginning with "u", the initial sound is not a vowel but the semi-consonant "[j]". In these cases, the indefinite article is "a", not "an" (e.g. "a unit"; "a useful book"; a "UFO"; etc).

5) We stayed in <u>an</u> hotel near the British museum.

We stayed in a hotel near the British museum.

The traditional use of "an" before "hotel" has been abandoned by the vast majority of contemporary English speakers.

OMISSION OF ARTICLE

6) I'm <u>only child</u>.

I'm an only child.

7) He is <u>working as barman</u>.

He is working as a barman.

8) Bertie <u>suffers from stammer</u>.

Bertie suffers from a stammer.

9) Before going to bed, I <u>read few pages</u> of a book.

Before going to bed, I read a few pages of a book.

"Few" means "not many" and is often translated with "pochi/poche"; "a few" has a more positive meaning and is frequently translated with "qualche" or "alcuni/alcune". However, see also 10) below.

10) There were only few students at the lesson yesterday.

There were only a few students at the lesson yesterday.

Note that after "only", even though there is a negative connotation, we use "a few" and not "few". See also 9) above.

11) I'm <u>working in gymnasium</u>.

I'm working in a gymnasium / in a gym.

Compare 8) in the chapter Definite Article.

MISUSE OF ARTICLE

12) My mother is 61; she is <u>a retired</u>.

My mother is 61; she is retired. / My mother is 61; she is a pensioner.

"Retired" is an adjective.

13) We see <u>a lots</u> of films together.

We see lots of films together. / We see a lot of films together.

"A" is singular, "lots" is plural.

14) My little sister was <u>a very good company</u>.

My little sister was very good company.

In this case "company" is uncountable. Compare "IKEA is a very good company to work for".

15) It deals with a subject of <u>a</u> great interest.

It deals with a subject of great interest.

USE OF DEFINITE ARTICLE WHERE INDEFINITE ARTICLE REQUIRED

16) I earned 20 euros <u>by the</u> week.

I earned 20 euros a week.

Compare the expressions: "three times a day", "£50 a kilo", "a hundred miles an hour".

"ONE"

17) I hope to work in the editorial sector <u>a</u> day.

I hope to work in the editorial sector one day.

18) I hope to return there <u>a</u> day.

I hope to return there one day.

19) You need a car to get from <u>a</u> town to another.

You need a car to get from one town to another.

EXERCISES

A. For each gap, decide whether to insert "a", "an", "one" or nothing:

1) My father is _____ retired now but he used to be _____ university professor.

2) She earns €7 _____ hour working as _____ hairdresser.

3) There were _____ lots of people and there was _____ lot of food.

4) I hope _____ day to see _____ UFO.

5) It's _____ honour to be invited to _____ house like this.

6) Being _____ only child is _____ unhappy experience for some.

7) She's _____ good company so I was happy to spend _____ few days with her.

8) _____ few people I know would not want to work for _____ company that treats its employees so well.

9) It's _____ useful gadget for _____ housewife to have.

10) My brother works in _____ gym four days _____ week.

11) Although there were _____ few opportunities for meeting people, from _____ day to the next I suddenly found myself with two new friends.

12) There are only _____ few biscuits left.

B. Write answers to the following questions, then ask the questions to your study partner and make a note of his/her answers:

1) What are the disadvantages of being an only child?

2) How much do you need to earn a month to get by?

3) Do you consider yourself good company?

4) Is there a company you'd particularly like to work for?

5) Have you ever worked as a waiter or a waitress?

6)) What are the advantages of being a pensioner?

Infinitive or -ing

1) I don't like <u>to live</u> in my hometown.

I don't like living in my hometown.

"Like" can be used with "to" + infinitive when referring to repeatable actions ("I like to get up late on Sundays") but not to permanent or ongoing states or actions ("I like being a foreigner here"; "Do you like working in this office?"). Often, as in 2) and 3) below, both forms are possible.

2) I like <u>teach</u> children new things.

I like teaching children new things. / I like to teach children new things.

3) I really like <u>sing</u>.

I really like singing. / I really like to sing.

"Like" is not used with the bare infinitive.

4) She would like <u>coming</u> with us.

She would like to come with us.

Although "-ing" is very occasionally used after "would like" ("You wouldn't like living here, believe me!"), the best strategy for language students is to always opt for "to" + infinitive.

5) The church contributed to <u>keep</u> people's souls pure.

The church contributed to keeping people's souls pure.

Note that in this case and in the examples 6) to 9) below, "to" is not a marker for the infinitive but a preposition; like all other prepositions, it is followed by the "–ing" form. Contrast with 10) below.

6) I was used to <u>live</u> in the city so I hated the countryside.

I was used to living in the city so I hated the countryside.

Distinguish "I used to live" ("vivevo/abitavo") from "I was used to living" ("ero abituato a vivere/ad abitare"). See also 7) and 8) below.

7) I am used to <u>cook</u> Italian dishes.

I am used to cooking Italian dishes.

8) She is not used to <u>speak</u> English.

She is not used to speaking English.

9) I look forward to <u>meet</u> him.
I look forward to meeting him.

10) I am not inclined to <u>eating</u> these things.
I am not inclined to eat these things.

11) I love music so I have never stopped <u>to play</u> the piano.
I love music so I have never stopped playing the piano.
Distinguish "stop + infinitive", which means "fermarsi per..." ("After driving for three hours we stopped to get some lunch"), from "stop + -ing", which means "smettere di...". See also 12) below.

12) In June I stopped <u>to attend</u> school.
In June I stopped attending school.

13) I wanted <u>become</u> a doctor.
I wanted to become a doctor.

14) <u>Have</u> a walk can be a relaxing activity.
Having a walk can be a relaxing activity.
When a verb is the subject/object (or part of the subject/object) of another verb, we generally use the -ing form. See also 15) to 18) below. For examples of exceptions, see 32) and 33) below.

15) I believe that writing is a little bit like <u>be</u> undressed.
I believe that writing is a little bit like being undressed.

16) Justice means <u>understand</u> what is wrong and what is right, then <u>punish</u> crimes and criminals.
Justice means understanding what is wrong and what is right, then punishing crimes and criminals.

17) She decides to do this even if it means <u>to break</u> the rules.
She decides to do this even if it means breaking the rules.

18) Happiness is not <u>live</u> in a big house but <u>have</u> a family that supports you and loves you.
Happiness is not living in a big house but having a family that supports you and loves you.

19) I avoid <u>to stay</u> alone.
I avoid staying / being alone.

20) I would risk <u>to lose</u> my job.
I would risk losing my job.

21) I would spend entire days <u>to watch</u> the rain fall.
I would spend entire days watching the rain fall.

22) I suggest <u>to come</u> to Italy during the spring.
I suggest coming to Italy during the spring. / I suggest [that] you come to Italy during the spring.

23) He didn't succeed <u>to do</u> it.
He didn't succeed in doing it.

24) I used to dream of <u>have</u> a sister or a brother.
I used to dream of having a sister or a brother.
After prepositions, use the "-ing" form of a verb. See also 5) to 8) above and 25) to 30) below.

25) The idea <u>to live</u> in the forest is fantastic.
The idea of living in the forest is fantastic.

26) I'm afraid <u>to not pass</u> my exams.
I'm afraid of not passing my exams. / I'm afraid I will not/won't pass my exams.

27) I always think before <u>to speak</u>.
I always think before speaking.

28) I was undecided between <u>study</u> psychology and languages.
I was undecided between studying psychology and languages.

29) Please go back to <u>sing</u>; acting is not your forte!
Please go back to singing; acting is not your forte!

30) I'm interested only <u>to find</u> what I lost.
I'm interested only in finding what I lost.

31) Did you have any problems <u>to find</u> it?
Did you have any problems finding it?

32) All they do is <u>playing</u> on their mobile phones.
All they do is play on their mobile phones.

33) My plans now are <u>enjoy</u> my new family and my new home.
My plans now are to enjoy my new family and my new home.

34) I will go to their office <u>trying</u> to sort it out.
I will go to their office to try to sort it out. / I will go to their office and try to sort it out.

35) I hope to work in a publishing house <u>having</u> a successful career.
I hope to work in a publishing house and [to] have a successful career.

36) I'll find the time <u>for reading</u> it tomorrow.
I'll find the time to read it tomorrow

37) This way we have an excuse not <u>going</u> to the party.
This way we have an excuse not to go to the party.

EXERCISES

A. Insert the appropriate form of the verb in each gap. In some cases there is more than one possibility.

1) I don't like (BE) _____ so tall: it's always difficult (FIND) _____ clothes that fit.

2) Where would you like (SIT) _____ ?

3) As a child, she always dreamed of (BECOME) _____ an architect.

4) I used to (PLAY) _____ a lot of football but I'm not used to (RUN) _____ around any more.

5) That whole morning he never stopped (TALK) _____ , not even (DRINK) _____ his coffee.

6) I'm not inclined to (BELIEVE) _____ anything that guy says.

7) (BRING UP) _____ children is never an easy task.

8) He's determined to do it even if it means (GET UP) _____ at five a.m. every day.

9) All they ever do is (CRITICISE) _____ .

10) Are you looking forward to (SPEND) _____ time with the in-laws?

11) Let's go back to (DO) _____ it the way we did before.

12) Did you have any problems (PARK) _____ in the city centre?

13) I could spend hours (LISTEN) _____ to her (SING) _____ .

B. Complete the sentences with an appropriate verb or verb phrase:

1) I love the idea of...

2) Where do you want...

3) You have to avoid...

4) She isn't prepared to risk...

5) He is afraid of...

6) I hope to graduate and...

7) They didn't succeed in...

8) Our plan is to...

9) Always wash your hands before...

10) I don't have time...

11) The guidebook suggests...

12) They are undecided between...

C. Write answers to the following questions, then ask the questions to your study partner and make a note of his/her answers:

1) What kinds of things are you used to eating?

2) What kinds of things did you use to eat as a child?

3) What are your plans for the next few months?

4) Is there a place you dream of living?

5) What kinds of clothes do you avoid wearing?

6) What does "relaxation" mean for you?

7) What are the things you are most looking forward to doing in the next few weeks?

Inventions

1) I'm writing to you about the <u>verbalization</u> of the credits for the course.
I'm writing to you about the registration of the credits for the course.

2) He has more strength than the <u>coetanous</u> boys.
He has more strength than other boys of his age.

3) It is too <u>malinconic</u> for me.
It is too melancholic/depressing for me.

4) My favourite <u>telefilm</u> is "Doctor Who".
My favourite TV series is "Doctor Who".

5) I felt <u>coinvolted</u> with excitement.
I felt excited. / I felt overcome with excitement.

6) I was very <u>impressioned</u> by this.
It made a strong impression on me. / This really shocked/upset me.

7) There is <u>ironism</u> in this.
There is irony in this.

8) The emperor ordered the soldiers to <u>lapidate</u> her.
The emperor ordered the soldiers to stone her.

9) My grandmother told stories of princesses, <u>mages</u> and fairies.
My grandmother told stories of princesses, wizards and fairies.

10) I work as a <u>barlady</u> at the weekend.
I work as a barmaid/bartender at the weekend.

11) It is my favourite <u>universitary</u> course.
It is my favourite university course.

12) Our schools are under <u>pression</u> because of the lack of funds.
Our schools are under pressure because of the lack of funds.

13) It is important to understand the <u>storic</u> context.
It is important to understand the historic context.

14) They were completely <u>alterated</u> by alcohol and drugs.
They were completely under the influence of alcohol and drugs.

15) Nobody should be <u>privated</u> of his personal identity.
Nobody should be deprived of his personal identity.

16) He was my favourite teacher because he <u>actualized</u> the subject.
He was my favourite teacher because he made the subject relevant to our times.

17) In my opinion it is <u>unuseful</u>.
In my opinion it is useless.

18) When I drink, I laugh and <u>overtalk</u>.
When I drink, I laugh and talk too much.

19) Lessons haven't begun because of the <u>restructuration</u> work.
Lessons haven't begun because of the renovation work.

20) We are <u>destinated</u> to be together.
We are destined/meant to be together.

21) It is one of many problems connected to <u>consumism</u>.
It is one of many problems connected to consumerism.

22) I forgot to water the plant and it was <u>arsed</u> in the sun.
I forgot to water the plant and it burned in the sun.
Although an invention in the sense intended here, the word "arsed" is occasionally used as a slightly vulgar alternative to "bothered" ("I should really be studying for my exam tomorrow but I can't be arsed"). Avoid it in exams and in polite conversation.

Like & As

USING "LIKE" WHERE "AS" IS REQUIRED
1) I sometimes work <u>like</u> a babysitter.
I sometimes work as a babysitter.

2) I really like her <u>like</u> an actress!
I really like her as an actress!

3) Some students perceive the teacher <u>like</u> a friend.
Some students perceive the teacher as a friend.

USING "AS" WHERE "LIKE" IS REQUIRED
4) I try to be strong, <u>as</u> her.
I try to be strong, like her.

5) <u>As</u> most of my peers, I have a lot of dreams.
Like most of my peers, I have a lot of dreams.

6) At the age of 6, I met Joanna and she became <u>as</u> a sister.
At the age of 6, I met Joanna and she became like a sister to me.

SUCH AS
7) I have visited a lot of Italian towns <u>as</u> Lecce, Gallipoli and Padua.
I have visited a lot of Italian towns such as Lecce, Gallipoli and Padua.

8) The houses (<u>as</u> Chatsworth) are extraordinary.
The houses (such as Chatsworth) are extraordinary.

using "as" when not required
9) I consider myself <u>as</u> a meditative person.
I consider myself a meditative person.

10) He considers me <u>as</u> a friend.
He considers me a friend.
Alternatively: "He sees me as a friend".

CONFUSING "LOOK" AND "LOOK LIKE"

11) She looks a witch!

She looks like a witch!

Use "look like" before a noun.

12) It looks like difficult.

It looks difficult.

Use "look" before an adjective.

MISTRANSLATING "SEMBRARE"

13) When they are sleeping, they seem little angels.

When they are sleeping, they look like little angels.

"Seem" and "seem like" are often used in preference to "look" and "look like" when the speaker wants to emphasise the idea that the appearance is or may be misleading ("It seemed like a good idea at the time [but it wasn't!]"; "It seems okay but I think we should get it checked anyway").

14) From the way you describe him, he seems a gangster.

From the way you describe him, he sounds like a gangster.

"Sound" and "sound like" are often used in preference to "look" and "look like" when the speaker's impression is based on what he/she has read or heard rather than seen.

OTHER

15) I didn't feel of doing it.

I didn't feel like doing it.

16) As they were pasture animals, the women are left neglected at home.

As if they were pasture animals, the women are left neglected at home.

EXERCISES

A. Insert "like", "as" or nothing into each gap to complete the sentences:

1) _____ most teenagers, he doesn't always see eye to eye with his parents.

2) She occasionally works _____ a waitress at weekends.

3) He wants to be an accountant, _____ his father.

4) Qualities such _____ reliability and thoroughness are essential for this job.

5) I admire him _____ a writer but I don't like him _____ a person.

6) He has always been _____ a brother to me.

7) Do you consider her _____ a friend?

8) I consider myself _____ a tolerant person.

9) It sounds _____ a wonderful place but it looks _____ expensive.

10) She looks _____ her mother.

11) He treats her _____ if she were his housekeeper.

12) Do you feel _____ going out this evening?

B. Write answers to the following questions, then ask the questions to your study partner and make a note of his/her answers:

1) Do/Did you perceive any of your teachers at school as a friend?

2) Who do you most look like in your family?

3) What do you feel like eating right now?

4) How would you react if someone treated you as if you were their housekeeper.

5) From what you have read and heard, how does life in London sound?

Mispronunciations

1) I have to go to <u>chair</u> practice.
I have to go to choir practice.

2) Jessica was <u>working</u> in the street with her sister yesterday evening.
Jessica was walking in the street with her sister yesterday evening.

3) Do you like <u>The Jets</u>?
Do you like jazz?
"Jazz" rhymes with "has".

4) I'm <u>suing</u> his trousers.
I'm sewing his trousers.
The verb "to sue" means "fare causa [a]".

5) She only ate about one <u>turd</u> of the pizza.
She only ate about one third of the pizza.
"Turd" is a slightly vulgar slang term for a piece of excrement ("You've just stepped in a dog turd, darling").

6) Can you give me the recipe for the <u>deep</u>?
Can you give me the recipe for the dip?

7) I will show you the <u>spacemen</u> we used in the experiment.
I will show you the specimen we used in the experiment.

*Compare the different pronunciations of these words by listening to the audio file at the following link: **https://soundcloud.com/paulandrewjarvis/mispronunciations-italian-mistakes?in=paulandrewjarvis/sets/english-mistakes-italians-make***

Missing Word

PRONOUNS

1) The book is controversial because is about gay marriage.

The book is controversial because <u>it</u> is about gay marriage.

We often omit a pronoun after "and", "but" and "or" when the subject of the following verb is the same as in the first clause ("She is good at skiing and is an excellent swimmer"; "He lives in Bologna but works in Modena"; "In the evenings I do yoga or drink beer") but not usually after other conjunctions. See also 2) and 3) below.

2) My mother couldn't work because was pregnant.

My mother couldn't work because <u>she</u> was pregnant.

3) If misunderstandings arise, can be remedied immediately.

If misunderstandings arise, <u>they</u> can be remedied immediately.

FEW

4) Everything has changed in these last years.

Everything has changed in these last <u>few</u> years.

5) In the last months I have studied a lot.

In the last <u>few</u> months I have studied a lot.

6) In the next years I would like to move to another country.

In the next <u>few</u> years I would like to move to another country.

PREPOSITIONS

7) I spend my evenings listening my favourite music.

I spend my evenings listening <u>to</u> my favourite music.

8) I don't remember what he said me.

I don't remember what he said <u>to</u> me.

9) I forgot water the plant.

I forgot <u>to</u> water the plant.

10) Look this photo!

Look <u>at</u> this photo!

11) I am living together three other girls.

I am living together <u>with</u> three other girls.

12) He learns that his father has been searching the Nazi officer who humiliated him in Auschwitz.

He learns that his father has been searching <u>for</u> the Nazi officer who humiliated him in Auschwitz.

Distinguish "to search someone" (= "perquisire": e.g. "The customs officers searched him because they were convinced he was carrying drugs") from "to search for someone/something" (= cercare in maniera approfondita").

13) He pays for his crime going to jail.

He pays for his crime <u>by</u> going to jail.

We use "by" + "-ing" to explain how something is done or achieved ("You turn it on by pushing this button"; "She passed the exam by studying seven days a week for six months").

OTHER

14) I played volley for ten years.

I played volley<u>ball</u> for ten years.

Note also that we say "basketball", not "basket", when talking about the sport.

15) I like the cinema very much and for this there are some films that I have seen many times.

I like the cinema very much and for this <u>reason</u> there are some films that I have seen many times.

The phrase "per questo", in the sense of "per questo motivo", is usually translated "for this reason".

16) I think there's too bureaucracy at this university.

I think there's too <u>much</u> bureaucracy at this university.

"Too" can be used before an adjective ("too difficult") or an adverb ("too fast") but before a noun it combines with "many" ("too many problems") if the noun is countable, and with "much" ("too much traffic") if the noun is uncountable. See also 16) to 18) in the chapter Adverbs.

17) When I was five years, we moved to another town.

When I was five years <u>old</u>, we moved to another town.

An alternative solution here would be to omit the word "years" ("When I was five, we moved to another town"). See also 1) in the chapter "Redundant Word".

18) He was the ex-coach of the Italian national.

He was the ex-coach of the Italian national <u>team</u>.

EXERCISES

A. Insert one word into each sentence so that it reads correctly. If you need help, a list of the missing words is provided at the end of the exercise.

1) When I was nine years, my father bought me a fishing rod.

2) He wasn't able to go to the concert because was sick.

3) Don't forget turn off the gas before you go away.

4) A rescue team has been searching the lost climbers for nearly two days now.

5) I haven't been able to go out much during the last weeks.

6) What kind of music do you listen?

7) If you hadn't been looking that girl, you wouldn't have crashed the car!

8) We have two small children and for this it is difficult for us to go out in the evenings.

9) He is working together his cousin.

10) Roberto Baggio played fifty-six times for the Italian national.

11) They resolved the problem calling in an expert.

12) We have decided against moving house: it's too hassle.

at   by   few   for   he   much   old   reason   team   to (2)   with

B. Write answers to the following questions, then ask the questions to your study partner and make a note of his/her answers:

1) Have you forgotten to do anything recently?

2) Who do you think is the best player ever to have appeared for the Italian national team?

3) Can you think of anything you have avoided doing recently because it was too much hassle?

4) What kind of music do you listen to?

5) How much has your life changed in the last few years?

Mistranslations

1) My father is a doctor. My mother, <u>instead</u> is an <u>employee</u>.
My father is a doctor. My mother, on the other hand, is a clerical worker. / My father is a doctor while my mother is a clerical worker.

2) I used to argue with my brother. <u>On the contrary</u>, I used to get on well with my cousins.
I used to argue with my brother. On the other hand, I used to get on well with my cousins.
To introduce a simple contrast, use "on the other hand"; "on the contrary" is used, often in the Italian sense of "anzi", to affirm that the truth is diametrically opposed to what has been said, or to correct a misapprehension ("English is not as easy as some people think; on the contrary, it's very difficult").

3) I really hope to <u>realise this dream</u>.
I really hope this dream will come true / I really hope to fulfil this ambition.

4) I like working with <u>children and guys</u>.
I like working with children and young people.
The term "guys" (like "sons", "brothers", "uncles" and "nephews") is generally used to refer only to males. Occasionally, particularly in American English, the vocative/appellative form (often lengthened to "you guys") also includes females. See also 5) and 6) below.

5) Jane Eyre is adopted by her <u>uncles</u>.
Jane Eyre is adopted by her uncle and aunt.

6) In "Before Sunset" two <u>guys</u> meet on the train and fall in love.
In "Before Sunset" a guy and a girl meet on the train and fall in love.

7) I don't like <u>yellows</u>.
I don't like detective stories.

8) I worked with <u>ancients</u> in a rest home.
I worked with old people in a rest home.
See also 13) in the chapter False Friends.

9) I hope to become a journalist or a teacher or <u>however</u> to earn money doing what I love.

I hope to become a journalist or a teacher or in any case to earn money doing what I love.

10) This is the story's first <u>point of strength</u>.

This is the story's first strong point.

11) I <u>enjoyed a childhood of serenity</u>.

I had a quiet / an untroubled childhood.

12) <u>Here is me</u>!

Here I am!

13) He was not <u>of good humour</u> because his team had lost.

He was not in a good mood because his team had lost.

14) <u>For what concerns the other</u>, I don't like it.

As far as the other one is concerned, I don't like it.

15) <u>We charged our luggage</u> onto the ferry, and the ship left.

We loaded our luggage onto the ferry, and the ship left.

16) The supermarket is near there so <u>I can make a jump</u>.

The supermarket is near there so I can pop in.

17) Walking along the beach <u>offered me the possibility</u> to appreciate the colours.

Walking along the beach gave me the opportunity to appreciate the colours.

18) We had <u>friends in common</u>.

We had mutual friends.

See also 1) in the chapter Collocations.

19) I decided to enrol in the <u>Faculty of Letters</u>.

I decided to enrol in the Faculty of Arts.

20) I would <u>remain surprised</u> if that happened.

I would be surprised if that happened.

21) My mobile phone _did not have network_.
I had no signal on my mobile phone.

22) _Pay attention to_ the puddles!
Be careful of the puddles!
"To pay attention" usually means to listen carefully to or (less frequently) to carefully watch someone or something ("He wasn't paying attention when the teacher explained how to do it"; "It's important to pay attention during the safety demonstration").

23) Thanks to my parents, _I have never missed anything_.
Thanks to my parents, I have never wanted for anything.
The speaker here was trying to convey the sense of "non mi è mai mancato niente".

24) _April's fish!_
April fool!

25) _Public means of transport are_ not very good here.
Public transport is not very good here.

26) Perhaps you know a secret language I ignore.
Perhaps you know a secret language [that] I am ignorant of.
If you "ignore" someone or something, you deliberately take no notice of them or it ("She's been ignoring me all evening"; "The best way to deal with insults is to ignore them").

27) Now is the time of lunch.
Now it's time for lunch.

EXERCISES

A. Rewrite using the word or phrase provided:

1) Naples is big, noisy and chaotic. Siena, instead, is small and quiet. (ON THE OTHER HAND)
2) It's more a place for families and middle-aged couples than for guys. (YOUNG PEOPLE)
3) Maths is one of my points of strength. (STRONG POINTS)
4) This one is my favourite of all Conan Doyle's yellows. (DETECTIVE STORIES)

5) My uncles got married in 1995 and had their first child two years later. (UNCLE AND AUNT)

6) I'd like to go to Spain or Greece or however somewhere hot. (IN ANY CASE)

7) If your mother needs a hand, we can make a jump later this afternoon. (POP IN)

8) She had a bad day at work so she isn't of good humour. (IN A GOOD MOOD)

9) For what concerns my future, I would like to work in the field of publishing. (AS FAR AS...IS CONCERNED)

10) This job offered me the possibility to travel. (GAVE ME THE OPPORTUNITY)

11) Pay attention to the ice on the mountain roads. (BE CAREFUL OF)

12) I'm sorry but I couldn't call you because I didn't have network. (HAD NO SIGNAL ON MY PHONE)

B. Write answers to the following questions, then ask the questions to your study partner and make a note of his/her answers:

1) How many uncles and aunts do you have?

2) What was the last detective story you read?

3) What kind of opportunities does speaking good English give you?

4) What puts you in a good mood?

5) Realistically, which of your dreams might come true?

6) Do you ever play April fool's jokes on your friends?

7) What are your strong points?

8) How much contact do you have with old people?

Modals

CAN, BE ABLE TO, MAY, MIGHT
1) They <u>don't can</u> come.
They can't come.

2) I hope <u>to can</u> play it again one day.
I hope to be able to play it again one day.

3) I hope <u>I'll could</u> find a good job.
I hope I'll be able to find a good job.

4) <u>I wish I will</u> be able to do that.
I wish I could do that. / I hope I will be able to do that.

5) My curly hair <u>can</u> reflect my strange personality.
My curly hair may reflect my strange personality.
Use "may" and "might" rather than "can" and "could" to convey the idea of possibility. Note that "might" usually indicates a slimmer possibility than "may". See also 6) and 7) below.

6) If the girls come too, they can be interested in the shops.
If the girls come too, they may/might be interested in the shops.

7) Working in a bar could seem monotonous but it is easy to meet a lot of different people.
Working in a bar might seem monotonous but it is easy to meet a lot of different people.

8) She doesn't bear her neighbours.
She can't bear her neighbours.
Note that the verb "stand", which has a meaning synomous to "bear", is also used with "can/can't" ("How can you stand working for that horrible woman?").

9) They captured the snake and we could continue our visit [to the zoo].
They captured the snake and we were able to continue our visit [to the zoo].
Use "was/were able to" rather than "could" when referring to a single event. Compare "She could ski before she could walk". See also 10) below.

10) My dad found a new job and my mum could go back to work at the hospital.

My dad found a new job and my mum was able to go back to work at the hospital.

11) It was a very bad accident. We may have been killed.

It was a very bad accident. We could/might have been killed.

"May have" + past participle is used to convey the idea that a possibility still exists, as in: "She may have gone shopping" (for the moment we don't know whether she has or not).

MUST & HAVE TO

12) You <u>must to</u> see it!

You must see it!

13) You <u>don't must</u> touch that!

You mustn't touch that!

14) In England you <u>must</u> drive on the left.

In England you have to drive on the left.

We use "must" when the person speaking (or writing) is imposing the obligation ("You must finish your homework, children, before you go out to play!"). In other situations, we prefer "have to / has to"

15) You <u>mustn't</u> study English: you can do French if you prefer.

You don't have to study English: you can do French if you prefer.

"Mustn't" conveys the idea that something is prohibited ("You mustn't go in the deep end of the pool: it's dangerous"). "Don't have to / doesn't have to" mean that, as in this example, there is no obligation.

16) You <u>have not to</u> pay immediately.

You don't have to pay immediately.

17) This is why I<u>'ve to</u> learn English.

This is why I have to learn English. / This is why I've got to learn English

When "have" is used without "got" to express the idea of obligation, it is not abbreviated.

18) I missed the lesson because I <u>must went</u> to the hospital.

I missed the lesson because I had to go to the hospital.

19) I <u>had to</u> do an exam yesterday but I missed it because I was sick.

I was supposed to do an exam yesterday but I missed it because I was sick.

"Had to" is used for a past obligation that was fulfilled ("I had to do an exam yesterday and fortunately I passed"), "supposed to" for a past engagement that – as in this case – was not fulfilled.

SHOULD & OUGHT TO

20) You <u>should to</u> tell her

You should tell her. / You ought to tell her

"Should" and "ought to" are practically synonymous. See also 21) below.

21) You <u>ought speak</u> to him about it.

You ought to speak to him about it. / You should speak to him about it.

22) I <u>should did</u> it yesterday but I didn't have time.

I should have done it yesterday but I didn't have time.

23) He <u>should has</u> been more honest.

He should have been more honest.

EXERCISES

A. In each sentence underline one of the options in italics:

1) He *is not able / can't* speak German.

2) We hope to *be able to / can* go back there next summer.

3) I wish we *can / could* see each other more often.

4) It *can / may* snow tomorrow.

5) The exchange rate *could / might* not be as good next week.

6) Fortunately the rain stopped and I *was able to / could* finish the job.

7) We *may / might* easily have lost that match: the other team played really well.

8) You *have / 've* to press that button to start it.

9) She *must / has to* be at work by 9 o'clock every day.

10) We *don't have / have not* to decide immediately: we have a day or two to think it over.

11) You *don't have to / mustn't* touch that wire: it's dangerous!

12) You *don't have to / mustn't* have a car to get around here: the public transport is excellent.

B. Write answers to the following questions, then ask the questions to your study partner and make a note of his/her answers:

1) Is there anything you can't do that you wish you could?

2) What are the things people ought to do to protect the environment?

3) What time did you have to be at school/work/university yesterday?

4) What might have happened if Germany had won the Second World War?

5) Do you have to run any errands tomorrow?

6) Were you able to do Exercise A without making any mistakes?

7) What are the things you can't bear about Italy?

Negatives

1) I <u>couldn't do nothing</u> else.
I couldn't do anything else.

2) <u>Nobody has never</u> criticised it before.
Nobody has ever criticised it before.

3) <u>I don't have neither</u> the courage nor the strength to do it.
I don't have either the courage or the strength to do it. / I have neither the courage nor the strength to do it.

4) <u>No, there is anybody</u> there.
No, there is nobody there. / No, there isn't anybody there.
The term "any", although often used in negative expressions, is not itself negative. See also 5) below.

5) I would like to see an NBA basketball game but unfortunately <u>there will be any</u> in summertime.
I would like to see an NBA basketball game but unfortunately there will not be any in summertime.

6) I hope <u>the price is no high</u>.
I hope the price is not high.

7) <u>There will be no enough</u> space for your baggage.
There will not be enough space for your baggage.

8) I have <u>not idea</u>.
I have no idea.

9) Unfortunately <u>no one of my friends</u> likes this kind of music.
Unfortunately none of my friends like/likes this kind of music.
Note that although some traditionalists insist on using a singular verb with "none", most native speakers prefer the plural. See also 10) below.

10) At my school there were some bullies <u>but none dangerous</u>.
At my school there were some bullies but none [of them] was/were dangerous.

11) <u>No one mother</u> would do that.

No mother would do that.

12) He <u>doesn't can</u> do it.

He can't do it.

Most modal verbs form their negative by the simple addition of "not" or "n't" ("may not"; "mightn't"; "mustn't"; etc). See also the chapter Modals.

13) We <u>don't see</u> the sea from our balcony.

We can't see the sea from our balcony.

Just as in the affirmative and interrogative English speakers usually use "can" with verbs of the senses ("I can hear a strange noise"; "Can you smell that?"), so in the negative they use "can't" ("She can't hear very well"; "I can't feel my toes"). The corresponding past tense forms are "could" ("We could see the Eiffel Tower from our hotel") and "couldn't" ("You couldn't hear a thing with the music playing so loud"). See also 4) and 5) in the chapter Tenses – Present, *and 14) below.*

14) I <u>don't find</u> the webpage you told me about.

I can't find the webpage you told me about.

15) She realises that she <u>hasn't to</u> do it alone.

She realises that she doesn't have to do it alone.

"Haven't/hasn't", like "haven't got / hasn't got", are alternatives to "don't have / doesn't have" when the verb indicates possession ("He hasn't [got] time") but not when it describes an action ("They don't have lunch at home on Saturdays") or when, as in this case, it expresses the idea of obligation

16) <u>Both Thursday and Friday I wouldn't</u> have any problems.

I wouldn't have any problems either Thursday or Friday.

17) I feel <u>no more</u> embarrassed.

I don't feel embarrassed any more. / I no longer feel embarrassed.

See also 8) in the chapter Adverbs *and 18) below.*

18) He is <u>no more</u> alone.

He is not alone any more. / He is no longer alone.

19) We did a lot of reckless things that <u>I prefer don't</u> write here.

We did a lot of reckless things that I prefer not to write about here.

The negative infinitive is "not to + verb stem".

20) Her husband <u>seems not really</u> in love with her.

Her husband doesn't seem [to be] really in love with her.

21) <u>I think no</u>.

I don't think so.

EXERCISES

A. In each sentence underline one of the options in italics:

1) *Anybody / Nobody* has ever spoken to me like that before.

2) All things considered, it was *not / no* expensive.

3) I'm afraid there will *not / no* be enough time to go to the other museum.

4) There is *not / no* indication of how long it will take.

5) *None / No one* of my brothers went to university.

6) *No one / No* referee would have given a penalty for that.

7) I *can't / don't* hear what she is saying.

8) He says he *can't / doesn't* find it anywhere.

9) I would prefer *not / not to* go.

10) We had the worst seats in the house: we *didn't / couldn't* even see the stage properly.

B. Using the word provided in block capitals and the number of words indicated in brackets, complete each unfinished sentence so that it means exactly the same as the one above:

1) There wasn't anybody with us who could speak Chinese.

There _____ with us who could speak Chinese. (2) NOBODY

2) There isn't either a theatre or a cinema in the town.

There _____ a cinema in the town. (5) IS

3) They no longer work here.

They _____ more. (4) DON'T

4) The best strategy is to say nothing.

The best strategy is _____ . (4) NOT

5) I would offer you some cake but unfortunately it has all gone.

I would offer you some cake but unfortunately _____ left. (3) THERE

Numbers

1) My name is Francesco and I'm <u>twenty years ago</u>.
My name is Francesco and I'm twenty years old.

2) I have <u>19 years</u>.
I am 19. / I am 19 years old.

3) I am <u>tall 1.55 cm</u>.
I am one metre, fifty-five [centimetres] [tall].

4) The tunnel is <u>long three kilometres</u>.
The tunnel is three kilometres long.

5) My birthday is the <u>three September</u>.
SPOKEN ENGLISH: My birthday is on the third of September. / My birthday is on September the third.
WRITTEN ENGLISH: My birthday is on 3rd September. / My birthday is on September 3rd.
Note that in American English the preferred spoken form is "on September third".

6) I was born in <u>the 1989</u>.
I was born in 1989.

7) My bag weighed <u>half past eight kilos</u>.
My bag weighed eight and a half kilos.

8) We had lunch <u>at one and a half</u>.
We had lunch at half past one.

9) They have <u>only a child</u>.
They have only one child.
Use "one" in preference to "a/an" when there is an explicit or implicit contrast with a larger number ("We just have one car now but we used to have two").

10) <u>The things I like are two</u>.
There are two things I like.

11) The population is about five thousand <u>and</u> five hundred people.

The population is about five thousand, five hundred [people].

Use "and" only directly before the numbers 1-99 ("three hundred and sixty-six"; "two thousand and one"; etc).

12) My train is <u>at three and twenty</u>.

My train is at twenty past three. / My train is at three twenty.

13) <u>63,5%</u> of 2.000 is <u>1.270</u>.

63.5% of 2,000 is 1,270.

EXERCISES

A. Reorder the words to form complete sentences:

1) tall / is / metre / seventy-five / she / one

_____ .

2) boat / thirty / long / the / is / metres.

_____ .

3) two / kilometres / twenty-two / London / thousand / three / and / from / hundred / is / Lecce

_____ .

4) and / weighed / the / three / a / baby / half / kilos

_____ .

5) two / hates / there / she / things / are

_____ .

6) only / objection / I / one / have

_____ .

7) the / January / nineteen / born / nineteenth / on / she / ninety-two / of / was

_____ .

B. Write answers to the following questions, then ask the questions to your study partner and make a note of his/her answers:

1) How old are you?

2) How tall are you?

3) When is your birthday?

4) What year were you born?

5 What time do you usually have dinner?

6) What is the population of the town where you live?

7) What is 50% of 3, 000?

Of or 's or nothing

MISUSE OF "OF"

1) I worked as <u>an assistant of a barber</u>.
I worked as a barber's assistant.

2) I'll publish it in <u>the newspaper of the university</u>.
I'll publish it in the university newspaper.

3) He is <u>an engineer of telecommunications</u>.
He is a telecommunications engineer.

4) In the summer the town is <u>a destination of tourism</u>.
In the summer the town is a tourist destination.

5) I took the entrance test for <u>the academy of the police</u>.
I took the entrance test for the police academy.

6) In the four <u>months of summer</u> she works.
In the four summer months she works.

7) Next month we're leaving for London for <u>a week of holiday</u>.
Next month we're leaving for London for a week's holiday.
The form "week[s] of holiday" is generally used in more formal contexts ("Employees are entitled to four weeks of holiday a year").

8) I'm <u>a student of the course of</u> intermediate English.
I'm a student from/on the intermediate English course.

MISUSE OF APOSTROPHE FORM

9) I like <u>all the Agatha Christie's books</u>.
I like all the Agatha Christie books. / I like all Agatha Christie's books.

10) It was <u>a passion's summer</u>.
It was a summer of passion.

11) In this film I like the <u>dialogue's pace</u>.
In this film I like the pace of the dialogues.

12) She talked about <u>a Leopardi's poem</u>.
She talked about a poem of Leopardi's. / She talked about a Leopardi poem.

13) I could astonish you with <u>my catechism's knowledge</u>.
I could astonish you with my knowledge of catechism.

14) I'm a student <u>at Bari's university</u>.
I'm a student at the University of Bari / at Bari University.

15) He was <u>a law's student</u>.
He was a law student. / He was a student of law.

16) I was born <u>in Martina Franca, Taranto's province</u>, in 1992.
I was born in Martina Franca, in the province of Taranto, in 1992.

17) I chose the <u>literature's course</u> because I like to write and to read.
I chose the literature course because I like to write and to read.

18) It is <u>a 1997's film</u>.
It is a 1997 film.

19) When I was fifteen I broke <u>my knee's ligament</u>.
When I was fifteen I broke my knee ligament.

20) My brother works in <u>the Mulino Bianco's factory</u>.
My brother works in the Mulino Bianco factory.

21) The story is narrated with <u>the flashback's technique</u>.
The story is narrated with the flashback technique.

22) My cousin invited me to <u>a classical music's concert</u>.
My cousin invited me to a classical music concert.

23) I began attending <u>piano's lessons</u>.
I began attending piano lessons.

24) This is a problem for many <u>animal's species</u>.
This is a problem for many animal species.

25) After university <u>my life's style</u> changed.
After university my lifestyle changed.

26) I didn't like <u>the blood's scenes</u>.
I didn't like the scenes with blood.

27) Mr Collins, <u>the clumsy Elizabeth Bennet's cousin</u>.
Mr Collins, Elizabeth Bennet's clumsy cousin.

OMISSION OF "OF" OR APOSTROPHE FORM
28) You feel like one of <u>a black sheep flock</u>.
You feel like one of a flock of black sheep.

29) Please don't forget to bring me <u>the photocopy of the last Thursday lesson</u>.
Please don't forget to bring me the photocopy of/from last Thursday's lesson.

30) My father started a business: he opened <u>a butcher shop</u>.
My father started a business: he opened a butcher's shop.

EXERCISES

A. Combine the pairs of words in italics using "of", an apostrophe, both or neither. If necessary, invert.
1) Which is your favourite *play/Shakespeare*?
2) The road was blocked by a *herd/cows*.
3) How are your *lessons/Latin* going?
4) I'm thinking of doing a *course/yoga*.
5) It is faster than the *speed/light*.
6) I'm very envious! She has a *month/holiday*.
7) He has an impressive *knowledge/computers*.
8) Some of my best friends are *students/engineering*.
9) These animals hibernate during the *months/winter*.
10) We're going to a *concert/Springsteen* in Milan next month.
11) We went on a school trip to the *factory/Fiat* when we were teenagers.
12) My *muscles/stomach* are aching after all that exercise.

B. Write answers to the following questions, then ask the questions to your study partner and make a note of his/her answers:

1) What are the most interesting tourist destinations near where you live?

2) How are the summer months different from the winter months for you?

3) Which is your favourite Disney film?

4) How many weeks' holiday do you get a year?

5) Have you ever written for a school or university newspaper?

6) Has your lifestyle changed in the last five years?

7) Which animal species do you think it is most important to protect?

Participles

1) The film is <u>setted</u> in the present.
The film is set in the present.

2) The tomatoes are <u>cutted</u> into small pieces.
The tomatoes are cut into small pieces.

3) I haven't <u>saw</u> any films this week.
I haven't seen any films this week.

4) It was a horrible school, where the girls were <u>beated</u>.
It was a horrible school, where the girls were beaten.

5) My friend had already <u>rent</u> this flat the year before.
My friend had already rented this flat the year before.

6) The little city is very <u>crowd</u> during the summer.
The little city is very crowded during the summer.

7) I am <u>interesting</u> in cooking.
I am interested in cooking.
Distinguish "interesting" ("interessante") from "interested" ("interessato"). See also 8) and 9) below.

8) At the moment I'm <u>concentrated</u> on my studies.
At the moment I'm concentrating on my studies.

9) I went to a school <u>specialised</u> in scientific subjects.
I went to a school specialising / that specialises in scientific subjects.

10) They have been <u>marrying</u> for thirty years.
They have been married for thirty years.

11) I've been <u>ridden</u> since 2005.
I've been riding since 2005.

12) How long have you been <u>lived</u> in this house?
How long have you been living in this house?

13) Please find in attachment three files containing drafts of the work.

Please find attached three files containing drafts of the work.

This is a rare example of separation of verb and object. See the chapter Word Order.

14) It is the story of Elizabeth, just dumped by her boyfriend.

It is the story of Elizabeth, who has just been dumped by her boyfriend.

See also 14) and 15) in the chapter Relatives.

15) There were houses that seemed built with marzipan.

There were houses that seemed to have been built [out] of marzipan.

16) I'm writing to apologise to you for being disappeared.

I'm writing to apologise to you for disappearing. / I'm writing to apologise to you for having disappeared.

17) Seen how cold it is today, we could make some hot chocolate.

Seeing how cold it is today, we could make some hot chocolate.

18) Finished high school, I started studying Law.

After finishing high school, I started studying Law.

EXERCISES

A. In each sentence, write the correct form of the verb provided:

1) Juventus have only been (BEAT) _____ twice so far this season.

2) I want to apologise for not (REPLY) _____ sooner.

3) Where is the book (SET) _____ ?

4) He is not going out much at the moment; he is (CONCENTRATE) _____ on preparing his next exam.

5) How long have your parents been (MARRY) _____ ?

6) Are you (INTEREST) _____ in modern art?

7) (SEE) _____ as you have time on your hands, you could help me with this.

8) After (COMPLETE) _____ the course, she found a job immediately.

9) My nephew goes to a school (SPECIALISE) _____ in classical subjects.

10) Please find (ATTACH) _____ my CV.

B. Write answers to the following questions, then ask the questions to your study partner and make a note of his/her answers:

1) Where is your favourite film set?

2) Have you had to apologise for anything recently?

3) What kind of school did you go to?

4) How hard are you concentrating at the moment?

5) What kinds of things are you interested in?

Phrasal Verbs

1) The candle is <u>turned on</u> by the waiter when you sit down.

The candle is lit by the waiter when you sit down. / The waiter lights the candle when you sit down.

Lights are "turned on" (and "turned off"); candles are "lit" (and "blown out").

2) You can't <u>come back</u> into the past.

You can't go back to/into the past.

See also 52) in the chapter Wrong Word.

3) I've got the car; I can <u>get you off</u> at the station if you like.

I've got the car; I can drop you off at the station if you like.

4) She is trying to <u>get up</u> smoking.

She is trying to give up smoking.

See also 16) below.

5) I used to <u>get on my cousin</u>.

I used to get on with my cousin.

"Get on" in the sense of "andare d'accordo" is intransitive. As a transitive verb it means "salire su".

6) It is not easy to <u>get by</u> difficulties like this.

It is not easy to get round difficulties like this.

7) I wasn't able to <u>switch on it</u>.

I wasn't able to switch it on.

With "switch on", as with a number of phrasal verbs, the position of the object noun is flexible ("I wasn't able to switch on my phone"; "I wasn't able to switch my phone on") while the position of the object pronoun is not.

8) If I weren't so lazy, I would <u>end up</u> my projects much more quickly.

If I weren't so lazy, I would finish off my projects much more quickly.

The verb "end up" is intransitive; it is often found with "in + noun" ("How did you end up in Bari?") or an "-ing form" ("We ended up going to another restaurant").

9) Boyfriends <u>take away</u> a lot of time.

Boyfriends take up a lot of time.

10) He sees her, <u>goes next to</u> her and kisses her.

He sees her, goes up to her and kisses her.

11) I am trying to <u>make out</u> why he behaved in that way.

I am trying to work out why he behaved in that way.

12) He <u>hangs on</u> the phone and leaves.

He hangs up the phone and leaves.

13) I enjoy reading because I can <u>leave out</u> my problems and imagine other worlds.

I enjoy reading because I can put my problems to one side and imagine other worlds.

The verb "leave out" means to omit, either by choice or accident ("I think you should leave out this paragraph"; "When you make the guest list, be sure not to leave anybody out").

14) If we don't do this, pollution will <u>grow up</u>.

If we don't do this, pollution will increase.

"Grow up" is usually only used with reference to children ("What do you want to be when you grow up?"). See also 15) below.

15) When I <u>grow</u>, I want to be a teacher.

When I grow up, I want to be a teacher.

Distinguish "grow", which means to become physically bigger, from "grow up", which means to become an adult.

16) I had to <u>renounce</u> dance when I started high school.

I had to give up dance when I started high school.

17) We <u>made</u> shows at the theatre in my town.

We put on shows at the theatre in my town.

18) I worked but I was unable to <u>accumulate</u> the money I needed to buy the car.

I worked but I was unable to save up the money I needed to buy the car.

19) I missed the last lesson and I have to <u>recover</u> it.

I missed the last lesson and I have to make it up.

20) After we go to the museum we can <u>pass</u> to other things like visiting the Dolmen.
After we go to the museum we can move on to other things like visiting the Dolmen.

21) In this area, a car is the best way to <u>move</u>.
In this area, a car is the best way to get around.

22) She put her toys in the bath and <u>opened</u> the water.
She put her toys in the bath and turned on the water.

23) We would <u>take</u> the task of overall coordination of the project.
We would take on the task of overall coordination of the project.

24) Many animal species will <u>die</u>.
Many animal species will die out.

25) The second one <u>results</u> more interesting.
The second one turns out to be more interesting.

26) We are going <u>out</u> for five days at the end of April.
We are going away for five days at the end of April.
Distinguish "go out", which means "uscire [di casa]", from "go away", which means "andare fuori città".

EXERCISES

A. In each sentence underline the most suitable of the options in italics:

1) I had a row with my girlfriend on the phone and she hung *out / over / down / up* on me.
2) The local theatre company is putting *out / on / up / in* Macbeth next month.
3) A guy in the street came *off / up / through / behind* to me and asked me for money.
4) I can't work *out / over / in / at* how to open this thing.
5) The children take *out / in / up / down* a lot of my time these days.
6) We don't get many holidays but we always go *out / outside / in / away* for a few days in August.
7) It sounded interesting but it turned *up / in / out / over* to be a disappointment.
8) Who do you get *up / on / through / for* best with?

9) Giving *over / off / into / up* cigarettes was the hardest thing I have ever done.

10) Students have to make *up / out / down / on* any lessons they miss.

11) Where do you want me to drop you *for / to / off / away*?

12) I'm too busy to take *after / on / through / at* any more work at the moment.

B. Write answers to the following questions, then ask the questions to your study partner and make a note of his/her answers:

1) Who do you get on best with?

2) What are the things you could never give up?

3) Are you saving up for anything at the moment?

4) Have you ever been involved in putting on a show?

5) If you could go back into the past, which historical period would you choose to visit?

6) How do you usually get around?

7) Are you going away anywhere in the next few weeks?

8) How often do you go out?

Possessives

1) During <u>the</u> free time I read a lot.
During my free time I read a lot.

2) I hope to find <u>the</u> soul-mate soon.
I hope to find my soul-mate soon.

3) I spent <u>the</u> university years living with other students.
I spent my university years living with other students.

4) I'm going to stay there for two months; <u>at return</u>, I will do the exam.
I'm going to stay there for two months; on my return, I will do the exam.

5) I don't think my weekend was much better than <u>your</u>.
I don't think my weekend was much better than yours.
*Distinguish the possessive adjective "your" from the possessive pronoun "yours".
Note also the corresponding distinction between: "my" and "mine"; "her" and
"hers"; "our" and "ours"; "their" and "theirs".*

6) She continues <u>his</u> journey and finally arrives in New York.
She continues her journey and finally arrives in New York.

7) This is a problem for <u>the</u> our future.
This is a problem for our future.

8) I hope to be happy with <u>a my family</u>.
I hope to be happy with a family of my own.

9) I haven't <u>a my house</u>.
I haven't a house of my own.

10) In <u>this his work</u> he shows the society of the 16th century.
In this work of his, he shows the society of the 16th century.

11) We stayed with <u>friends of us</u>.
We stayed with friends of ours.
*Similarly: "a colleague of mine"; "a habit of his"; "cousins of theirs"; etc. See also 12)
below.*

12) I look forward to meeting these <u>relatives of your</u>.
I look forward to meeting these relatives of yours.

13) Molfetta is famous for <u>his</u> harbour.
Molfetta is famous for its harbour.

14) I want to visit Japan and <u>his</u> capital, Tokyo.
I want to visit Japan and its capital, Tokyo.

15) I liked London and <u>it's</u> nightlife.
I liked London and its nightlife.
"It's" means "it is" ("It's a wonderful place") or "it has" ("It's got a lot of art galleries").

16) She <u>corrected me the homework</u>.
She corrected my homework [for me].

EXERCISES

A. Identify and correct the errors in the following sentences:
1) I banged the head yesterday and it's still hurting me.
2) She suffered regularly from morning sickness during his pregnancy.
3) I don't think mine is as good as your.
4) A colleague of us is trying to resolve the problem.
5) Living alone has it's advantages.
6) Can you correct me these exercises?
7) We were impressed by London and all his parks.
8) He is saving up to buy a his house.
9) In this her letter she describes the house where she lived.
10) I'm going away for a week but at return I will call you.

B. Write answers to the following questions, then ask the questions to your study partner and make a note of his/her answers:
1) What do you do in your free time?
2) Have you met your soul-mate yet?
3) How important is it for you to have a house of your own?

4) What is your hometown famous for?

5) Have any of your friends got a more interesting life than yours?

Prepositions

ABOUT
1) Initially I was sad <u>of</u> this.

Initially I was sad about this.

The preposition "about" is used after many adjectives that describe an emotion (e.g. happy, sad, angry, worried, delighted, distressed, etc). See also 2) below.

2) Are you happy <u>for</u> the result of the match?

Are you happy about the result of the match?

Note that after "happy" and "delighted" we sometimes use "with" ("His boss isn't very happy with him at the moment"; "She is delighted with her new dress").

3) It is, in my opinion, the best thing <u>of</u> this job.

It is, in my opinion, the best thing about this job.

4) I started thinking <u>to study</u> philosophy.

I started thinking about studying philosophy.

We don't use the preposition "to" after the verb "think".

5) He thinks only <u>to</u> himself.

He thinks only about/of himself.

AFTER
6) <u>Since</u> that first lesson, I started to cook for my family.

After that first lesson, I started to cook for my family.

AT
7) She is <u>to</u> school today.

She is at school today.

8) I'm working as a waitress <u>in the weekend</u>.

I'm working as a waitress at weekends.

9) <u>In</u> the same time, I worked as a part-time accountant.

At the same time, I worked as a part-time accountant.

10) <u>In this moment</u> I am very happy.

At the moment I am very happy.

BECAUSE OF

11) I remember how boring English lessons used to be, not <u>for</u> the subject itself but <u>for</u> my teacher.

I remember how boring English lessons used to be, not because of the subject itself but because of my teacher.

BETWEEN

12) The aim is to improve relations <u>among</u> the four institutions.

The aim is to improve relations between the four institutions.

Use "between" in preference to "among" when referring to people or things that are seen as individual or separate from each other.

BY

13) The film is inspired <u>from</u> a real historical character.

The film is inspired by a real historical character.

14) It was inspired <u>from</u> a book.

It was inspired by a book.

15) The project must be submitted <u>until</u> 30th of April.

The project must be submitted by 30th of April.

16) I hope to graduate <u>within</u> next October.

I hope to graduate by next October.

17) We came <u>with the</u> car.

We came by car.

Note also: "We came in the car".

FOR

18) I'm leaving <u>to</u> Barcelona tomorrow.

I'm leaving for Barcelona tomorrow.

19) He accepted the job and left <u>to</u> Japan.

He accepted the job and left for Japan.

20) I asked him an autograph.
I asked him for an autograph.

21) How much did you pay the car?
How much did you pay for the car?
You "pay for" an item or service; you "pay" the person or company that is selling or providing it ("We paid him for the work he did").

22) I never felt the need of it.
I never felt the need for it.

23) There is a need of balance.
There is a need for balance.

24) We couldn't understand the reason of his behaviour.
We couldn't understand the reason for his behaviour.

25) In my opinion, the banks themselves are responsible of this crisis
In my opinion, the banks themselves are responsible for this crisis

26) We have been together since a year.
We have been together for a year.
Used together with the present perfect in the sense of the Italian "da" or "dal", "for" indicates duration ("for three hours"; "for years"; "for a long time") while "since" indicates the point at which the action began ("since 5th January"; "since Christmas"; "since I was a child").

FROM
27) I received many presents by my grandfather.
I received many presents from my grandfather.

28) Pollution of the seas is often caused by oil of ships.
Pollution of the seas is often caused by oil from ships.

IN
29) About the first film, I liked the final scene most.
In the first film, I liked the final scene most.
Note also: "As regards the first film, I liked the final scene most".

30) I took part <u>to</u> a lot of tournaments.
I took part in a lot of tournaments.

31) I'm <u>at</u> the first year of the course.
I'm in the first year of the course.

32) I don't write <u>on</u> my diary every day.
I don't write in my diary every day.

33) She read about it <u>on</u> the newspaper.
She read about it in the newspaper.

34) I was born in Foggia, a city <u>of</u> Puglia.
I was born in Foggia, a city in Puglia.

35) I used to pretend to be the characters <u>of</u> the movies that I watched.
I used to pretend to be the characters in the movies that I watched.

36) It has the best beaches <u>of</u> the region.
It has the best beaches in the region.
See also 18) in the chapter Comparatives & Superlatives.

37) This increase <u>of</u> temperature is probably due to global warming.
This increase in temperature is probably due to global warming.

INTO
38) He bursts <u>in</u> the room.
He bursts into the room.

39) You need to cut these <u>in</u> very small pieces.
You need to cut these into very small pieces.

40) We moved <u>in</u> this house in 2005.
We moved into this house in 2005.

OF
41) <u>Between</u> the two, I prefer the first.
Of the two, I prefer the first.

42) What do you think <u>about</u> the new prime minister?

What do you think of the new prime minister?

Use "think of" when talking about an opinion.

ON

43) It depends <u>by</u> your point of view.

It depends on your point of view.

44) We spent the whole day <u>in</u> the beach.

We spent the whole day on the beach.

OPPOSITE

45) Our first house was <u>in front of</u> the hospital.

Our first house was opposite the hospital.

"In front of" usually translates "davanti a", not "di fronte a".

SINCE

46) My parents recorded it some years ago and <u>from</u> then I have seen it five or six times.

My parents recorded it some years ago and since then I have seen it five or six times.

TO

47) He invented a machine <u>for</u> decipher codes.

He invented a machine to decipher codes.

When used before an infinitive to describe purpose, the Italian "per" is generally translated with "to". See also 48) and 49) below.

48) I applied to join the Air Force <u>for</u> study medicine.

I applied to join the Air Force to study medicine.

49) She fights <u>for</u> assert her own identity.

She fights to assert her own identity.

50) When I was ten we returned <u>in</u> Taranto.

When I was ten we returned to Taranto.

51) Five years later they moved <u>in</u> Italy [from America].
Five years later they moved to Italy.

52) My first trip out Italy was <u>in</u> Romania.
My first trip outside Italy was to Romania.

53) He is married <u>with</u> another woman.
He is married to another woman.

54) I have been engaged <u>with</u> my boyfriend since 2009.
I have been engaged to my boyfriend since 2009.

55) Welcome <u>in</u> Bari!
Welcome to Bari!

WITH
56) Her obsession <u>of</u> perfection drives her.
Her obsession with perfection drives her.

57) I fell in love <u>of</u> a classmate at primary school.
I fell in love with a classmate at primary school.

58) I'm satisfied <u>of</u> my decision.
I'm satisfied with my decision.

59) We used a method involving interviews <u>to</u> experts.
We used a method involving interviews with experts.

WITHIN
60) You must finish it <u>by</u> three days.
You must finish it within three days.

NO PREPOSITION REQUIRED
61) Ask <u>to</u> them to come.
Ask them to come.

62) What time did you arrive <u>at</u> home?
What time did you arrive home?

63) When he returned to home, his wife was not there.
When he returned home, his wife was not there.

64) In these days most people in Western Europe have cars and mobile phones.
These days most people in Western Europe have cars and mobile phones.

65) For first, I think you should visit the Colosseum.
First, I think you should visit the Colosseum.

EXERCISES

A. Insert a preposition, if required, into each gap:

1) She was engaged _____ Vito but ended up getting married _____ Nicola.

2) The Queen is returning _____ London this afternoon and leaving _____ Scotland next week.

3) Who has he fallen in love _____ this time?

4) She doesn't think much _____ the present she got _____ her brother-in-law.

5) I've been thinking _____ when we first moved _____ this house.

6) The boss says she is very satisfied _____ my work and I'm happy _____ that.

7) You need to do this _____ the next three days: _____ Saturday at the latest.

8) The film is inspired _____ the true story of a woman who sells everything she has _____ pay _____ medical treatment.

9) She reminds me _____ a character _____ a film I saw _____ the weekend.

10) I asked _____ them _____ confirmation that they will all be leaving _____ the same time.

11) It depends _____ whether you think there is a real need _____ it.

12) I read _____ a magazine that, _____ the two, she was the one more obsessed _____ money.

B. Write answers to the following questions, then ask the questions to your study partner and make a note of his/her answers:

1) How are you feeling at the moment?

2) What's the best thing about living in Italy?

3) Where was your first trip abroad to?

4) What do you think of your prime minister?

5) Is there a character in a film that you identify with in any way?

6) Have you ever asked anyone for an autograph?

7) When did you move into the house you are now living in?

8) What do you do at weekends?

Pronunciations

Mother tongue pronunciations (British English) of the words listed in this chapter can be found at the following link:
https://soundcloud.com/paulandrewjarvis/pronunciations-italian-mistakes?in=paulandrewjarvis/sets/english-mistakes-italians-make

DIFFICULT VOWEL SOUNDS

1) air   bear   mayor   <u>par</u>ents   rare   spare   their

The vowel sound in the above words is the same as that in "there". Distinguish "mayor" ("sindaco") from "major" ("maggiore"); the latter rhymes with "wager".

2) earth   fur   hurt   stir   word   world   worse   worst

The vowel sound in the above words is the same as that in "her".

3) board   bought   saw   taught   war

The vowel sound in the above words is the same as that in "four".

4) manage   minute   pocket   women   village

In all of these words the second vowel is unstressed and pronounced like that in "big".

"SILENT" LETTERS

5) advised   breathed   called   composed   concerned
danced   filled   happened   mentioned   planned
proved   ruined   stayed   talked   warned

The "e" of the "-ed" suffix for the past simple and past participle is pronounced only after the letters "d" and "t" ("needed"; "avoided"; "wanted"; "wasted"; etc).

6) altered   considered   flattered   murdered
ordered   preferred   remembered   wondered

Listen and note how all of these words have a whole syllable less than if you Italianise the pronunciation.

7) could   should   would   folk   half   talk   walk

Avoid pronouncing the "l" in all of these words.

8) biscuit   build   building   built   guilt   guilty
Avoid pronouncing the "u" in all of these words.

9) climb   climbed   climbing   dumb   lamb   numb   thumb   tomb
Avoid pronouncing the "b" in all of these words.

10) bruise   cruise   fruit   juice   suit
Avoid pronouncing the "i" in all of these words. Be careful with "suite", which rhymes with "feet".

11) honest   honesty   honestly   honour
honoured   honourable   hour   hourly
Avoid pronouncing the "h" in all of these words.

12) answer   answered   answering   sword
Avoid pronouncing the "w" in these words. "Answer" rhymes with "dancer"

13) iron   ironed   ironing   tired
Avoid pronouncing the "r" in these words. "Iron" rhymes with "lion".

TRICKY STRESS
14) afternoon   available   Catholic   characteristic   colleague
comfortable   development   engineer   environment   industry
management   necessary   necessity   performance
*Write down problem words in a notebook and mark the primary stress for each in the way that will best help you to remember it (after<u>noon</u>, afterNOON, after**noon**, after*noon*, etc).*

15) canal   control   correct   hotel   police   report   supply   technique
Note that in all these words the stress is on the second syllable.

CONTRACTING SYLLABLES
16) breakfast   certificate   chocolate   colour   consider
cupboard   favourite   literature   occasional   occurred
particular   purpose   supposed   surface   temperature
Try slightly overemphasising the stressed syllables and relaxing your mouth for the unstressed syllables.

PROBLEM "C"

17) accident   cease   circumstances   recipe   science   success

EXTRA [j] SOUND

18) accumulate   formula   future   pure   unit   tube

PROBLEM PAIRS & SETS

19) height / weight

"Height" rhymes with "white"; "weight" rhymes with "late".

20) it / hit / eat / heat

Record your own pronunciation of these four words and compare it to the pronunciation at the audio link.

21) law / low

"Law" rhymes with "more"; "low" rhymes with "go".

22) sixteen / sixty

Stress "sixteen" on the second syllable, "sixty" on the first. The same principle can be applied to thirteen/thirty, fourteen/forty, etc. See also 21) below.

23) thir**teen**th / **thir**tieth

As with 18) above, record your own pronunciation of these two words and compare it to the pronunciation at the audio link. Make the task easier by stressing the syllables highlighted in bold.

24) though / through / thought / thorough

"Though" rhymes with "go"; "through" rhymes with "do"; "thought" rhymes with "port"; "thorough" rhymes with "borough".

25) Tuesday / Thursday

One strategy for remembering which is which is to memorise the sequence "Tuesday-Wednesday-Thursday".

26) weather / water

"Weather" rhymes with "together"; "water" rhymes with "daughter".

27) work / walk

"Work" rhymes with "Turk"; "walk" rhymes with "fork".

EXERCISES

A. Write the sentences you hear dictated at the following link:
https://soundcloud.com/paulandrewjarvis/dictation-pronunciations-italian-mistakes?in=paulandrewjarvis/sets/english-mistakes-italians-make

B. Check your answers using the key at the back of the book. Listen again to the dictated sentences as you read through the answers.

C. Write answers to the following questions, then ask the questions to your study partner and make a note of his/her answers:
1) What height and weight are you?
2) Do you ever have fruit juice or biscuits for breakfast?
3) What literature were you taught at school?
4) How concerned are you about the earth and the environment?
5) What's your favourite building in the world?
6) How thoroughly have you thought through your plans for the future?
7) How honest do you consider your colleagues?
8) What's the worst thing that's happened in Italy recently?

Questions

1) <u>What is</u>?

What is it?

The pronoun is also necessary in questions like "Where is it?", "Where are they?", "Who is it?", "What are they?, etc. See also 2) below and 4) in the chapter Impersonal "it".

2) <u>Is correct</u>?

Is it correct?

3) <u>Why schools are closed</u> on Saturdays?

Why are schools closed on Saturdays?

4) Where <u>are you come</u> from?

Where are you from? / Where do you come from?

5) <u>Do you have got</u> a car?

Have you got a car? / Do you have a car?

6) How do you <u>go</u> to university?

How do you get to university?

7) <u>Which</u> is your phone number?

What is your phone number?

"Which" is used in preference to "what" when the number of possibilities is limited in some way ("Which of these is your office number?").

8) <u>Which is your height</u>?

What height are you?

9) <u>How much are you tall</u>?/ <u>How much tall</u> are you?

How tall are you?

10) <u>What time you left</u> home this morning?

What time did you leave home this morning?

11) <u>What could do a man</u>?

What could a man do?

12) <u>What will you do this evening</u>?
What are you doing this evening?

13) What <u>do you make cry</u>?
What makes you cry?
When the subject of a question is "what...", "who", "which...", "how many...", or "how much...", the interrogative verb is formed in the same way as the affirmative ("Who lives here?" "Anna lives here"; "Which team played better?" "Real Madrid played better"; "How many children are coming to the party?" "Thirty children are coming"; etc). See also 14) and 15) below.

14) Which relatives <u>are they going</u> to the wedding?
Which relatives are going to the wedding?

15) How many <u>people did they vote</u>?
How many people voted?

16) What <u>did happen</u>?
What happened?
We only use "What did happen?" (to express a meaning along the lines of "Che cosa è successo veramente allora?") when the original "What happened?" question has not been answered satisfactorily: "Okay, so if they are lying about the whole episode, what did happen?". Note that in cases like this, the auxiliary verb is pronounced with a strong emphasis.

17) <u>How many time</u> have you been studying English?
How long have you been studying English?
Distinguish "How many times?" ("Quante volte?") from "How long" ("Da/Per quanto tempo?").

18) How I can <u>say in English "concorso"</u>?
How can I say "concorso" in English? / How do you say "concorso" in English?
This is an example of how in English we tend to avoid separating the verb from its object. See also the chapter Word Order.

19) <u>What means</u>?
What does it mean?

20) <u>How can I do to</u> contact him?
How can I contact him? / How do/can I go about contacting him?

21) You are there from 12 to 1.30, <u>isn't it</u>?

You are there from 12 to 1.30, aren't you?

Use "isn't it" as a tag question only to refer back to "it is / it's" in the main clause ("It's very hot today, isn't it?").

22) They will not be angry, <u>are they</u>?

They will not be angry, will they?

EXERCISES

A. Insert one word into each question so that it reads correctly, then ask the questions to your study partner and make a note of his/her answers:

1) What you doing tomorrow evening?

2) How long have you living in Catania?

3) How many times have you been Venice?

4) You are Italian, aren't?

5) How you get to work?

6) How do I about getting a new passport?

B. Write the questions:

1) _____ ?

It's me. Let me in!

2) _____ ?

I'm from Sicily.

3) _____ ?

Yes, she has a Mercedes.

4) _____ ?

She left the office about half past five this evening.

5) _____ ?

Nothing happened.

6) _____ ?

About thirty people came.

7) _____ ?

It means "errore".

8) _____ ?

He is one metre, eighty-two.

Redundant Word

1) I cried every morning until the age of seven <u>years</u>.
I cried every morning until the age of seven.

2) It is about 20 kilometres <u>far</u> from Taranto.
It is about 20 kilometres from Taranto.

3) I preferred <u>more</u> the second one.
I preferred the second one.
Alternatively: "I liked the second one more".

4) I find it <u>aesthetically</u> beautiful.
I find it beautiful.

5) No <u>one</u> doctor has been able to help him.
No doctor has been able to help him.
"No one" is a pronoun; the adjective is "no". See also 10) in the chapter Negatives.

6) I'm studying Arabic <u>language</u>.
I'm studying Arabic.

7) I would like to learn Spanish <u>language</u> and move to Spain.
I would like to learn Spanish and move to Spain.

8) Despite <u>of</u> everything, I did it.
Despite everything, I did it.
*"Despite" is synonymous with "in spite of" ("In spite of everything, I did it"). See also
9) below and 10) in the chapter* Conjunctions.

9) She succeeded despite <u>of</u> the difficulties.
She succeeded despite the difficulties.
Alternatively: "She succeeded in spite of the difficulties".

10) My friend told <u>to</u> me about this place.
My friend told me about this place.

11) It gives <u>to</u> me a sense of freedom.
It gives me a sense of freedom.

12) When I returned <u>to</u> home, I spent the rest of the day crying.
When I returned home, I spent the rest of the day crying.

13) Sometimes we need <u>of</u> other people.
Sometimes we need other people.

14) I have never supported <u>for</u> a particular team.
I have never supported a particular team.

15) I discussed <u>about</u> ebooks with the publisher.
I discussed ebooks with the publisher.

16) <u>At</u> what time do you get up?
What time do you get up?
The use of "at" is theoretically possible with "what time?" but native speakers nearly always omit it.

17) I am going there <u>for</u> to do some research.
I am going there to do some research.
To translate the Italian "per" before an infinitive, simply use "to". See also 47) to 49) in the Chapter Prepositions.

18) Here you are <u>my homework</u>.
Here you are.
Alternatively: "Here is my homework".

19) My parents are <u>two</u> doctors.
My parents are doctors.
Alternatively: "My parents are both doctors".

20) My mother, Silvia, <u>she</u> is 49.
My mother, Silvia, is 49.

EXERCISES

A. Remove the unnecessary word from each sentence:
1) When I was seven years, my parents divorced.
2) Our house is three kilometres far from the sea.

3) I like the sea but my girlfriend prefers more the mountains.

4) She is studying Chinese language.

5) He continued playing despite of his injury.

6) They gave to me a gift voucher for my birthday.

7) You will need of more than one.

8) What time are you going to home this evening?

9) We would like to discuss about this problem with a lawyer.

10) She is saving up for to pay for a training course.

11) Her parents are two teachers.

12) Their son, Marco, he is an engineer.

B. Remove the unnecessary word from each of the questions:

1) How far is the town where you live distant from the sea?

2) What kinds of things do you tend not to discuss about with your family?

3) What team do you support for?

4) What the languages have you studied?

5) Are you studying English for to improve your job prospects or for other reasons?

C. Write answers to the questions in Exercise B, then ask the questions to your study partner and make a note of his/her answers.

Reflexives

OMISSION OF PRONOUN

1) <u>I enjoyed a lot</u> at the party.

I enjoyed myself a lot at the party.

"Enjoyed" usually requires an object (compare "I enjoyed the party a lot"). An exception is the recent use of "Enjoy!", which is commonly used by waiting staff in restaurants.

STANDARD PRONOUN WHERE REFLEXIVE IS REQUIRED

2) <u>I could talk about me</u> for hours.

I could talk about myself for hours.

3) <u>Take care of you</u>.

Take care of yourself.

REFLEXIVE PRONOUN WHERE NO PRONOUN IS REQUIRED

4) It is about a woman and man who <u>meet themselves</u> on a train.

It is about a woman and man who meet on a train.

5) When they <u>separate themselves</u>, they make a deal.

When they separate, they make a deal.

EACH OTHER

6) They <u>know themselves</u> and then fall in love.

They get to know each other and then fall in love.

7) <u>We didn't see us</u> for a year.

We didn't see each other for a year.

8) <u>My parents started to argue between them</u> and then decided to split up.

My parents started to argue [with each other] and then decided to split up.

IMPORTING ITALIAN REFLEXIVE INTO ENGLISH

9) I <u>identify myself</u> with this character.

I identify with this character.

10) I hope to <u>graduate me</u> next year.
I hope to graduate next year.

11) When I get stressed out, I try to <u>relax me</u>.
When I get stressed out, I try to relax.

12) I am going to buy a house with my boyfriend and I would like to <u>marry me</u>.
I am going to buy a house with my boyfriend and I would like to marry / to get married.

13) I <u>enrolled me</u> at the university.
I enrolled at the university.

14) At eighteen I decided to <u>matriculate me</u> at the Faculty of Literature.
At eighteen I decided to enrol at the Faculty of Literature.
See also 51) in the Chapter Wrong Word.

OTHER
15) I didn't have the courage to <u>declare myself</u>.
I didn't have the courage to tell her/him about my feelings.

16) They are all trying to <u>fulfil theirselves</u>.
They are all trying to fulfil themselves.

17) I liked the book so much I decided to <u>write by myself some stories</u>.
I liked the book so much I decided to write some stories myself.
"By myself" means "alone" ("I live by myself") or "without help from others" ("I did it all by myself, Mummy!").

EXERCISES

A. In each sentence underline one of the options in italics:
1) Look after *you / yourself*!
2) Did you *enjoy yourselves / enjoy*?
3) We first *met ourselves / met* at university.
4) You should try to *relax you / relax* more.
5) I get the impression you don't like talking about *you / yourself*.

6) They *got to know each other / got to know* quite well over the following weeks.

7) His parents *separated themselves / separated* when he was still a toddler.

8) We *haven't seen each other / haven't seen* since primary school.

9) Readers will not find it easy to *identify themselves / identify* with the hero of the story.

10) She is going to *graduate her / graduate* next July.

11) They are always arguing *between / with* each other.

12) Our plan is to *marry us / marry* some time next year.

B. Write answers to the following questions, then ask the questions to your study partner and make a note of his/her answers:

1) When did you last really enjoy yourself?

2) Do you think you will ever marry?

3) How do you like to relax?

4) How often do you talk about yourself?

5) Do people in your family argue a lot?

Relatives

BASICS

1) I have a sister, Sara, <u>which</u> is sixteen.

I have a sister, Sara, who is sixteen.

We don't use "which" to refer to people. See also) below.

2) She didn't want to tell me <u>who's</u> fault it was.

She didn't want to tell me whose fault it was.

Distinguish "who's", which means "who is" ("Who's coming to the party?") or "who has" ("Who's drunk my beer?"), from "whose", which means "of who/whom". Note that "who's" and "whose" are pronounced the same and, like many homophones (compare "your" and "you're"), are often confused even by native speakers when they write.

3) I have a little dog that <u>he</u> is 8 years old.

I have a little dog that is 8 years old.

In this sentence, the relative "that" is the subject of the verb "is".

4) In my town there wasn't <u>a school where to go</u>.

In my town there wasn't a school [that] I could go to. / In my town there wasn't a school where I could go.

OVERELABORATING

5) He is a person <u>to whom</u> you can always talk.

He is a person [who/whom/that] you can always talk to.

The relative pronoun can usually be omitted when it is the object of the following verb. Note that the form "whom" is increasingly rare, particularly in spoken English.

6) That is the man <u>to whom</u> she got married.

That is the man [who/that] she got married to.

7) I would like to receive the course materials <u>of which</u> you spoke to us.

I would like to receive the course materials [that/which] you spoke to us about.

8) This is the reason <u>for which</u> I would recommend them.

This is the reason [why] I would recommend them.

DIFFERENT STRUCTURE REQUIRED IN ENGLISH

9) It is the first country in the world <u>which produces</u> all its energy from renewable sources.

It is the first country in the world to produce all its energy from renewable sources.

10) We need to find <u>a place where to park</u>.

We need to find somewhere to park. / We need to find a place to park.

11) I will buy <u>a house where live</u> with my family.

I will buy a house to live in with my family. / I will buy a house where I can live with my family.

12) You can see the sun <u>that shines</u> on the sea.

You can see the sun shining on the sea.

13) My father wanted <u>that I studied</u> medicine.

My father wanted me to study medicine.

Note that we use the same structure with "would like/would have liked" and "expect" ("My father would have liked me to study medicine"; "My father expected me to study medicine").

OMISSION OF NECESSARY RELATIVE

14) I have a sister older than me.

I have a sister who is older than me.

15) We need to reduce <u>emissions of CO$_2$, damaging</u> for our health.

We need to reduce emissions of CO$_2$, which are damaging for our health.

NON-DEFINING CLAUSES

16) Thanks to her, I discovered jazz, <u>that</u>'s still my favourite kind of music.

Thanks to her, I discovered jazz, which is still my favourite kind of music.

We don't use "that" at the beginning of a non-defining clause. It is a possible alternative to "which" or "who" at the beginning of a defining clause ("This music reminds me of the jazz that you were listening to yesterday"). See also the following examples.

17) The jacket is green <u>that</u> is my favourite colour.

The jacket is green, which is my favourite colour.

18) I go to concerts with my boyfriend, that likes the same music as me.

I go to concerts with my boyfriend, who likes the same music as me.

19) She meets her only friend, that will die young.

She meets her only friend, who will die young.

TRANSLATING "CHI"

20) Only who really loves her could do this.

Only someone who really loves her could do this.

21) Who wants to come must tell me now.

Anyone who wants to come must tell me now.

22) The most important thing is being loved and appreciated by who really knows you.

The most important thing is being loved and appreciated by those who really know you.

"QUELLO CHE"

23) He tells us to avoid only that we don't want to do.

He tells us to avoid only what we don't want to do.

24) I prefer to write because if I speak I say less than half that I want to say.

I prefer to write because if I speak I say less than half [of] what I want to say.

EXERCISES

A. Match each sentence beginning to a suitable ending:

1) I have a very good friend...

2) Have you met the guys...

3) Anyone who requires a vegetarian meal...

4) In the photo there is a baby...

5) My parents would prefer...

6) There's a very good reason...

7) We're looking for a place...

8) This is the very house...

9) She can't decide...

10) Have you any idea...

11) They are talking about politics,...

a) ...why we ask you to do this.

b) ...which is something I hate.

c) ...me to stay in Italy.

d) ...to do up ourselves.

e) ...who works in Pavia.

f) ...what she wants.

g) ...[that] she has hired to do the job?

h) ...should let us know beforehand.

i) ...where he was born.

j) ...whose jacket this is?

k) ...crawling across a lawn.

B. Write answers to the following questions, then ask the questions to your study partner and make a note of his/her answers:

1) In what kinds of situations do you tend not to say what you think?

2) Can you recommend a place to spend a relaxing weekend?

3) What was the first film or TV series [that] you saw in English?

4) Who are the people [that] you can always ask for help?

5) Is there a specific reason [why] you are reading this book?

6) How would you like / would you have liked your teachers at school to be different?

Singular & Plural Forms

1) When I was <u>a children</u>, I loved hip-hop dance.
When I was a child, I loved hip-hop dance.

2) I'm <u>a fans</u> of Inter.
I'm a fan of Inter. / I am an Inter fan.

3) I prefer to wear <u>a jeans</u> and t-shirt.
I prefer to wear jeans and a t-shirt.
If you wish to emphasise that you are referring to a single item of clothing, use "a pair of jeans".

4) I collect <u>DVD</u>.
I collect DVDS.

5) <u>The people was</u> warm and helpful.
The people were warm and helpful.

6) I live with <u>others friends</u>.
I live with other friends.
English adjectives are invariable. See also 7) and 8) below.

7) I was impressed by how <u>others European</u> societies work.
I was impressed by how other European societies work.

8) I used to play in the street with <u>my twins cousins</u>.
I used to play in the street with my twin cousins.

9) <u>Every Fridays</u> I used to play in the orchestra.
Every Friday I used to play in the orchestra.
Like "ogni", "every" is used only with singular nouns. See also 10) below.

10) I like <u>every kind of books</u>.
I like every kind of book. / I like all kinds of books.

11) I really appreciate <u>this kind of suggestions</u>.
I really appreciate this kind of suggestion. / I really appreciate these kinds of suggestions.

12) He took me to kindergarten <u>all mornings</u>.
He took me to kindergarten every morning.
"All morning" can be used to translate "tutta la mattinata".

13) The husband and wife quarrel <u>all times</u>.
The husband and wife quarrel all the time.

14) This is <u>one of my hobby</u>.
This is one of my hobbies.

15) <u>One of this choice</u> was difficult.
One of these choices was difficult.

16) It is <u>one of the most beautiful scene</u> in the history of Italian cinema.
It is one of the most beautiful scenes in the history of Italian cinema.

17) <u>On Saturday I usually</u> go out with my friends.
On Saturdays I usually go out with my friends.
"On Saturday" is usually used to refer to next Saturday or last Saturday depending on the context.

18) It is the perfect way to meet <u>new persons</u>.
It is the perfect way to meet new people.

19) I'll always <u>be friend with</u> them.
I'll always be friends with them.

20) I <u>made friend with</u> a girl who was five, like me.
I made friends with a girl who was five, like me.

21) I'm not <u>interested in politic</u>.
I'm not interested in politics.
Although it looks like a plural, "politics" is a singular noun.

22) I haven't <u>any brother or sister</u>.
I haven't any brothers or sisters.

23) I didn't know <u>any girl</u>, only boys.
I didn't know any girls, only boys.

24) The <u>guilties</u> were never punished.

The guilty were never punished.

Plural nouns derived from adjectives usually adopt the adjectives' invariable form ("Her music appeals to young and old alike"; "The blind are often unable to participate in activities like this").

25) My father met my mother when <u>they were teenager</u>.

My father met my mother when they were teenagers.

26) We both know <u>what we want to do in our life</u>.

We both know what we want to do in our lives.

While it is true that each individual has only one life, in this case the subject is plural and therefore more than one life is being referred to.

27) We caught <u>a lot of fishes</u>.

We caught a lot of fish.

The names of many fish also remain unchanged in the plural ("We bought three salmon, four mackerel and a couple of trout").

28) I work in <u>a shoes shop</u>.

I work in a shoe shop.

When a plural noun slots into the position of an adjective before another noun, it reverts to its singular form. See also 29) and 30) below.

29) I've always been <u>a films lover</u>.

I've always been a film lover.

30) She obliged me to do <u>a two weeks English course</u>.

She obliged me to do a two-week English course.

Compare "a ten-mile run", "a twelve-part series", "a five-kilo weight", etc.

31) I love dogs and my dream has always been to <u>open a kennel</u>.

I love dogs and my dream has always been to open a kennels.

"A kennel" is a small structure designed to house one dog. A place or business that can accommodate a number of dogs is "a kennels".

32) The time for those reforms were 20 years ago.

The time for those reforms was 20 years ago.

"Although "reforms" immediately precedes the verb, the actual subject is "The time for those reforms", which is singular.

EXERCISES

A. Correct the error in each sentence:

1) Most people doesn't like that kind of thing.
2) I have been friend with him for many years.
3) It was one of the scariest experience I have ever had.
4) Have you been to any concert recently?
5) I was a very active children.
6) She is a fans of Madonna.
7) How many DVD did you lend her?
8) People are always leaving their umbrella on the bus.
9) None of the others students passed the exam.
10) Our mission is simply to feed the hungries.
11) They own a five-metres boat.
12) The association meets every Wednesdays.

B. Write answers to the following questions, then ask the questions to your study partner and make a note of his/her answers:

1) How often do you buy DVDS?
2) Does politics play an important role in your life?
3) What time do you usually get up on Sundays?
4) How many pairs of jeans do you own?
5) Have you ever caught any fish?
6) What are the people like in the town where you live?

Some & Any

1) <u>Do you want</u>?

Do you want some? / Do you want one?

We use "some" in preference to "any" in questions where the existence of the thing or things referred to is not in doubt. Compare "That chocolate looks nice! Can I have some?" with "Have you got any chocolate?".

2) In Florence I visited a wonderful art gallery with <u>several</u> beautiful paintings.

In Florence I visited a wonderful art gallery with some / a number of beautiful paintings.

"Several" gives the sense of more than two but is usually understood to mean no more than four or five. One would expect a "wonderful" gallery to have more than "several" beautiful paintings.

3) I could have <u>avoided some quarrel</u>.

I could have avoided some quarrels.

When "qualche" is used in the sense of "alcuni/alcune", the noun following "some" in the English equivalent is plural.

4) I would like <u>to meet some Hollywood actor</u>.

I would like to meet a Hollywood actor. / I would like to meet some Hollywood actors.

"Some" is occasionally used with the singular form of a countable noun to mean "one" and to suggest that the speaker has no way of, or no interest in, identifying exactly the person or thing referred to ("Some idiot has broken the photocopier"; "They were talking about some disco they went to"). An exception is in exclamations, where "some" is often used to express the idea of "wonderful" ("Messi is some player!").

5) <u>Someone says</u> I don't look Italian because of my blond hair.

Some people say I don't look Italian because of my blond hair.

The term "someone" is only used to refer to a single person. See also 6) below.

6) <u>For most people it's weird but for someone</u> it's delightful.

For most people it's weird but for some it's delightful.

7) <u>In the last few years I have done some jobs</u>: babysitting, working in a bar, teaching children, etc.

In the last few years I have done various jobs: babysitting, working in a bar, teaching children, etc.

8) I think there is nothing better than <u>spending some hours</u> in a relaxing place.

I think there is nothing better than spending a few hours in a relaxing place.

9) In the last few years I have had <u>a couple of relationships with some girls</u>.

In the last few years I have had a couple of relationships with girls.

The use of "some" here would suggest that each relationship was with more than one girl, which is of course possible but not what the speaker intended.

10) I <u>haven't skeletons</u> in my cupboard.

I haven't any skeletons in my cupboard.

11) We would <u>appreciate every useful advice</u>.

We would appreciate any useful advice.

When the Italian "ogni" is used with the sense of "qualsiasi", it is usually translated with "any". See also 12) below.

12) It's very simple: <u>everyone can do it</u>.

It's very simple: anyone can do it.

When the Italian "tutti" is used in the sense of "chiunque", it is often translated with "anyone/anybody".

13) You can call me <u>anytime</u>.

You can call me any time.

14) <u>Have you planned any event</u> in October?

Have you planned an event / any events in October?

EXERCISES

A. In each sentence underline the more suitable of the options in italics:

1) Are there *some / any* rivers in Puglia?

2) That cake looks delicious! Can I have *some / any*?

3) This cheese is really good. *Would you like some / Would you like*?

4) We could spend *some / a few* hours looking round that art gallery you mentioned.

5) A spokesman said that *some / a number of* candidates were being considered for the post.

6) For the most part it's a very civilised place although you do meet some rude *person / people*.

7) Have you seen any good *film / films* recently?

8) The show was amazing: she is *some / any* singer!

9) *Someone uses / Some use* garlic in this recipe but we prefer it without.

10) There are *some / several* reasons why you can't go: firstly you're too young, secondly it's too expensive and thirdly it's dangerous.

B. Write answers to the following questions, then ask the questions to your study partner and make a note of his/her answers:

1) Have you planned any holidays over the next few months?

2) If you could spend a few hours in the company of a famous person, who would you choose?

3) Have you got any skeletons in your cupboard?

4) Who are the people that can call you any time?

5) Is there any advice you would give to tourists visiting your town for the first time?

Spellings

adress – **address**

Augoust – **August**

beatiful – **beautiful**

breackfast – **breakfast**

caracter/ carachter – **character**

choise – **choice**

cleaver – **clever**

costant – **constant**

difficolt – **difficult**

enjoied – **enjoyed**

exame – **exam**

faboulous – **fabulous**

gelous – **jealous**

healty – **healthy**

indipendence – **independence**

litterature – **literature**

Micheal – **Michael**

mounth – **month**

particolar - **particular**

phisical – **physical**

plaied – **played**

Pool – **Paul**

rappresenting – **representing**

shainess – **shyness**

somethink – **something**

studing – **studying**

sweetcase – **suitcase**

teatre – **theatre**

tipical – **typical**

tollerant – **tolerant**

whit/whith – **with**

affascinated – **fascinated**

Barcellona – **Barcelona**

belive – **believe**

bycicle - **bicycle**

childwood – **childhood**

cinic – **cynic**

confortable – **comfortable**

developped – **developed**

ecc. – **etc.**

esistence – **existence**

expecially – **especially**

foto – **photo**

granparents – **grandparents**

immagine – **imagine**

infact – **in fact**

mather – **mother**

mistery – **mystery**

partecipate – **participate**

peacefull – **peaceful**

phylosophy – **philosophy**

plaing – **playing**

psichology – **psychology**

Santa Clause – **Santa Claus**

semplified – **simplified**

speach – **speech**

suspance – **suspense**

Tanks! – **Thanks!**

theacher – **teacher**

togheter – **together**

tryed – **tried**

wich – **which**

1) Next month I'm <u>living</u> for England to do some research.
Next month I'm leaving for England to do some research.

2) It is <u>compost</u> of four parts.
It is composed of/made up of four parts.

3) He overcomes his <u>fair</u> of the sea.
He overcomes his fear of the sea.

4) My teacher has a long <u>bird</u>.
My teacher has a long beard.

5) Taranto is famous for its <u>muscles</u>.
Taranto is famous for its mussels.

6) The local community had to <u>except</u> the factory.
The local community had to accept the factory.

7) It was <u>past</u> down to me by my parents.
It was passed down to me by my parents.
Although "passed" and "past" are pronounced the same, they have different functions: "passed" is a verb ("She passed by this morning"; "He has passed all his exams now") while "past" is used as a noun ("She's living in the past"), an adjective ("I've been studying the past papers"), an adverb ("Who was the guy that just walked past?) or a preposition ("Will you be going past the station?").

EXERCISES

A. Correct the spellings by adding one letter to each word:
1) adress   2) beatiful   3) belive (*credere*)   4) costant   5) granparents   6) healty
7) studing (*studiando*)   8) tanks (*grazie*)   9) teatre   10) wich (*quale*)

B. Correct the spellings by removing one letter from each word:
1) August   2) breackfast   3) developped   4) exame   5) faboulous
6) immagine   7) mounth (*mese*)   8) peacefull   9) theacher   10) tollerant

C. Correct the spellings by changing a letter:
1) choise   2) confortable   3) difficolt   4) enjoied   5) expecially
6) indipendence   7) mistery   8) partecipate   9) phylosophy
10) psichology   11) somethink

D. Correct the spellings by moving one or more letters:
1) bycicle   2) carachter   3) Micheal   4) phisycal   5) togheter   6) whit

Tenses: Present

1) Please specify when it <u>start</u> and <u>finish</u>.
Please specify when it starts and finishes.

2) <u>My father don't</u> like the city.
My father doesn't like the city.

3) <u>How much costs</u> the whole holiday?
How much does the whole holiday cost?

4) From my bedroom window <u>I see</u> a park and another building.
From my bedroom window I can see a park and another building.
Verbs of the senses ("vedo", "sento", etc) are very often translated into English with "can" ("I can smell something burning"). See also 5) below and the chapters Modals *and* Negatives.

5) <u>I don't hear</u> what she is saying.
I can't hear what she is saying.

6) <u>I write you this letter</u> to tell you about our new project.
I am writing you this letter to tell you about our new project.

7) Fortunately <u>my phone line now works again</u>.
Fortunately my phone line is now working again.

8) She <u>thinks that he jokes</u> about this.
She thinks that he is joking about this.

9) <u>At the moment I enjoy</u> the university life.
At the moment I am enjoying the university life.

10) <u>I'm specialised</u> in it.
I specialise in it.

11) <u>I am agree</u>.
I agree.

12) My mother <u>is not agree</u> with me.
My mother does not agree with me. / My mother disagrees with me.

13) <u>I use to spend</u> my holidays at our cottage.

I [usually] spend my holidays at our cottage.

There is no present tense of the past form "used to". The idea of repetition or habit is implicit in the simple present verb and may be reinforced by the adverb "usually".
See also 14) below.

14) We support the same team so <u>we use to go</u> to the stadium together.

We support the same team so we [usually] go to the stadium together.

15) Do you <u>know where does he work</u>?

Do you know where he works?

The interrogative part of the question here is "Do you know?".

EXERCISES

A. In each sentence underline the more suitable of the options in italics:

1) One of my former students now *live / lives* in Liverpool.

2) Her children *don't / doesn't* eat meat.

3) What time does your lesson *finish / finishes*?

4) *Do you / Are you* agree with the proposal?

5) I *write / am writing* to you to inform you that I wish to end my subscription.

6) Why *do you look / are you looking* at me like that? *Is my face / My face is* dirty?

7) She *doesn't / can't* see very well without her glasses.

8) Can you ask her what *she wants / does she want*?

9) We *use to / usually* spend a month there in the summer.

B. Write answers to the following questions, then ask the questions to your study partner and make a note of his/her answers:

1) What can you see from your bedroom window?

2) Can you hear your neighbours through the walls of your house?

3) Are you enjoying life at the moment?

4) How do you usually spend your holidays?

5) Do you know what your best friend is doing right now?

6) Do you agree with the idea of shorter summer holidays for schools?

Tenses: Future Forms

1) One day I <u>will became</u> an editor.
One day I will become an editor.

2) <u>If I'll do</u> it, I'm sure that it will be very interesting.
If I do it, I'm sure that it will be very interesting.
In 1ˢᵗ conditional sentences, use the present simple in the "if" clause and the will/shall/'ll form in the main clause. See also 3) below and the chapter Conditionals.

3) I <u>don't</u> take offence if you offer me money for it.
I won't take offence if you offer me money for it.

4) <u>When we will graduate, we</u> are going to get married.
When we graduate, we are going to get married.
After temporal conjunctions, use the Present Simple to express a future sense. See also 5) below.

5) We will buy our own house <u>as soon as we will have</u> enough money.
We will buy our own house as soon as we have enough money.

6) <u>This Christmas I'll go to Rome</u> with my friends.
This Christmas I'm going to Rome with my friends. / This Christmas I'm going to go to Rome with my friends.
Use the Present Continuous in preference to the will/shall/'ll form to describe arrangements. See also 7), 8) and 9) below.

7) <u>On Sunday afternoon I'll go and see an art exhibition</u> at the Sala Murat.
On Sunday afternoon I'm going to see an art exhibition at the Sala Murat.

8) I can't come to the lesson <u>next Wednesday: I'll do an exam.</u>
I can't come to the lesson next Wednesday: I'm doing an exam.

9) <u>After the lesson I must meet a friend</u> for a coffee.
After the lesson I'm meeting a friend for a coffee.

10) <u>Tell me when I can find you and I come</u> and visit you.
Tell me when I can find you and I'll come and visit you.
To make a promise or an offer of help, use the will/shall/'ll form.

11) I think to telephone her this evening.

I think I will telephone her this evening.

In English we do not use the infinitive after the verb "think".

EXERCISES

A. In each sentence, write the correct form of the verb provided:

1) It will be difficult if you (NOT GET) _____ someone to help you.

2) You will be informed when your documents (BE) _____ ready.

3) As soon as we (HEAR) _____ from the lawyer, we will let you know.

4) We (MEET) _____ some friends in the Irish pub at half past eight this evening.

5) I think I (DO) _____ it now. I won't have time later.

6) She (GO) _____ back to Taranto to see her parents next weekend.

7) Don't worry: I (NOT BE) _____ angry if you don't finish in time.

B. Write answers to the following questions, then ask the questions to your study partner and make a note of his/her answers:

1) What are you doing next weekend?

2) Where do you think you will be this time next year?

3) What are you going to do after you finish school / graduate / retire?

4) If you get any free time this week, how will you spend it?

Tenses: Simple Past

1) I <u>don't was</u> happy.
I wasn't happy.

2) This is the reason <u>I chosen</u> it.
This is the reason I chose it.

3) At the age of seven <u>I begun</u> to read detective stories for children.
At the age of seven I began to read detective stories for children.

4) Two years later <u>she given</u> birth to my sister.
Two years later she gave birth to my sister.

5) My parents <u>teached</u> me the importance of courage.
My parents taught me the importance of courage.

6) I remember <u>a lesson I founded interesting</u>.
I remember a lesson I found interesting.
"Founded" is the past of the verb "to found" ("fondare"), not "to find".

7) It almost <u>costed</u> me my life.
It almost cost me my life.

8) I was in London when Princess Diana <u>deaded</u>.
I was in London when Princess Diana died.

9) I <u>didn't passed</u> the test.
I didn't pass the test.

10) <u>Did you succeeded</u>?
Did you succeed?

11) What time <u>did you left</u> this morning?
What time did you leave this morning?

12) When I was younger <u>I had got a canary and now I've got</u> a sea turtle.
When I was younger I had a canary and now I've got a sea turtle.
The past form of "have/has got" is simply "had". See also 13) below.

13) At first <u>I got difficulties</u>.
At first I had difficulties.

14) <u>At the age of six I have met</u> my best friend.
At the age of six I met my best friend.
We use the Simple Past rather than the Present Perfect if, as here, we specify when a finished action happened. See also 15) and 16) below.

15) <u>Before I came here, I have had</u> a lot of different working experiences.
Before I came here, I had a lot of different working experiences.

16) <u>When I was seventeen I have fallen</u> in love.
When I was seventeen I fell in love.

17) <u>The scene that I liked most has been</u> the last one.
The scene that I liked most was the last one.
We use the Simple Past rather than the Present Perfect when both speaker and interlocutor know when the action happened.

18) <u>The last book I have read</u> was Plato's "Symposium".
The last book I read was Plato's "Symposium".
Similarly: "I can't remember the last time I saw him"; "The last exam I did was not so easy".

19) <u>I've played volleyball for six years but I stopped</u> because of school.
I played volleyball for six years but I stopped because of school.
"I've played volleyball for six years" means that you are still playing ("gioco a pallavolo da sei anni").

20) I chose this kind of school because I <u>did want</u> to be able to communicate with people from all over the world.
I chose this kind of school because I wanted to be able to communicate with people from all over the world.
In the affirmative, did + verb stem is used to contradict a negative statement (- "Vito didn't want to go." - "That's not true: he did want to go.") or, in an exclamation, to give emphasis ("I did enjoy that party!"). It is not used as a simple alternative to the standard past tense form.

21) <u>Who has painted "Guernica"</u>?

Who painted "Guernica"?

Compare "Who wrote King Lear?"; "Who invented the telescope?"; "Who scored the winning goal?"; etc.

22) Who <u>did tell</u> you this?

Who told you this?

For an explanation, see 13) in the chapter Questions.

23) I <u>used to went</u> to the swimming pool twice a week.

I used to go to the swimming pool twice a week.

We never use a Simple Past form with "used to" although we often use one as an alternative to "used to + verb stem" ("I went to the swimming pool twice a week when I was a child").

24) <u>It's time I buy</u> a dictionary.

It's time I bought a dictionary.

25) Perhaps she <u>was thinking</u> it was a joke!

Perhaps she thought it was a joke!

26) My mother <u>is born</u> in Milan.

My mother was born in Milan.

EXERCISES

A. Correct the error in each sentence:

1) She doesn't was at school yesterday.

2) My father teached in a secondary school for twenty years.

3) I founded my watch in the pocket of my other jacket.

4) The wedding costed them a fortune.

5) He deaded before he finished composing his last symphony.

6) We chosen it because it seemed the best option at the time.

7) They both had got great difficulty understanding what he was saying.

8) We didn't managed to get there in time.

9) Where did you bought it?

10) When I was eleven, I have started doing guitar lessons.

11) The last film I have seen at the cinema was "Interstellar".

12) My friend used to came to my house every evening after school.

B. In each sentence, write the correct form of the verb provided:

1) Things (BECOME) _____ easier as time went by.

2) We (BEGIN) _____ going out together three and a half years ago.

3) Who (GIVE) _____ you permission to do that?

4) What time (YOU GET) _____ home last night?

5) My nose used to (BLEED) _____ every time I went up a mountain.

6) At the time I (THINK) _____ it was strange.

7) They (BE) _____ both born in Abruzzo.

8) It's time we (LEAVE) _____ .

9) We (LIVE) _____ there for eight years but then we (MOVE) _____ .

10) At the age of fifteen, I (JOIN) _____ a band.

C. Write answers to the following questions, then ask the questions to your study partner and make a note of his/her answers:

1) Where was your best friend born?

2) How often did you use to do sports activities at primary school?

3) What was the last book you read?

4) Did you have any pets when you were a child?

5) How old were you when you started school?

Tenses: Present Perfect & Past Perfect

PRESENT PERFECT SIMPLE
1) I'm become good at cooking.
I've become good at cooking.
The auxiliary verb for the Present Perfect is "have/has". See also 2) below.

2) The prisoners <u>are</u> been freed.
The prisoners have been freed.

3) How long <u>do you know</u> her?
How long have you known her?
To translate "da quanto tempo + presente/presente progressivo", use the present perfect (simple or continuous, depending on the situation), not the Simple Present or Present Continuous. See also 16) below.

4) I <u>live</u> in Carbonara since I was born.
I have lived in Carbonara since I was born.
In English we use the Present Perfect (simple or continuous, depending on the situation) + "for" (in the sense of "da") or "since" (in the sense of "da/dal/da quando") to describe the duration of an unfinished action or state. See also 5), 11) and 12) below.

5) Currently he <u>is</u> my boyfriend for five years.
He has now been my boyfriend for five years.

6) This is the third book they <u>write</u> together.
This is the third book they have written together.
See also 7) below.

7) Is it the first time you <u>are in</u> Bologna?
Is it the first time you have been to Bologna?

8) I haven't got any skeletons in my cupboard because I <u>had</u> buried them.
I haven't got any skeletons in my cupboard because I have buried them.

9) Unfortunately I <u>spent</u> all my money this month.

Unfortunately I have spent all my money this month.

With adverbs of time that include the present ("today"; "this year"; "these last few weeks"; etc), we generally prefer the Present Perfect to the Simple Past. See also 10) below.

10) In the last few years I <u>did</u> various jobs for them.

In the last few years I have done various jobs for them.

PRESENT PERFECT CONTINUOUS

11) I <u>wait</u> for you for forty minutes.

I have been waiting for you for forty minutes.

12) For twenty years I <u>am going</u> to Rome to visit my cousins.

For twenty years I have been going to Rome to visit my cousins.

13) These jobs <u>are</u> disappearing in recent years.

These jobs have been disappearing in recent years.

14) Unfortunately my mobile <u>doesn't work</u> since yesterday.

Unfortunately my mobile hasn't been working since yesterday.

15) How long <u>have you studying</u> English?

How long have you been studying English?

16) We have <u>gone</u> to that restaurant since 2006.

We have been going to that restaurant since 2006.

PAST PERFECT

17) I realised what I had <u>wrote</u>.

I realised what I had written.

18) They told me you had <u>forgot</u>.

They told me you had forgotten.

19) She cried for a week about what <u>was</u> happened.

She cried for a week about what had happened.

The auxiliary verb for the Past Perfect is always "had". See also 21) below.

20) She thought that my friend Giovanni <u>was</u> fallen in love with Roberta.

She thought that my friend Giovanni had fallen in love with Roberta.

21) My teacher thought I had done it but I <u>didn't</u>.

My teacher thought I had done it but I hadn't.

22) If I <u>have</u> known, I would have come.

If I had known, I would have come.

EXERCISES

A. In each sentence underline the more suitable of the options in italics:

1) She *is / has* become a first-rate photographer.

2) *Are / Have* the invitations all been sent out?

3) I *have had / have got* this teddy bear since I was three.

4) He has made excellent progress *this month / last month*.

5) Is it the first time you *do / have done* anything like this?

6) I *haven't / hadn't* eaten sea urchins before we tried them in that restaurant.

7) We *have gone / have been going* there for years: we love the place!

8) There isn't any ice cream left because your sister *has / had* eaten it all.

9) They *had / were* never been up a volcano until we took them to Etna.

10) If she *was / had* arrived earlier, she could have eaten with us.

11) I *realised / have realised* too late what I had done.

12) My mother thought my father had *forgot / forgotten* but he *didn't / hadn't*.

B. Write answers to the following questions, then ask the questions to your study partner and make a note of his/her answers:

1) How long have you lived in your house?

2) How much money have you spent this month?

3) How long have you been working on this exercise?

4) How many jobs have you done in the last few years?

5) If you hadn't decided to study English today, how would you have spent the time.

Tenses: Conditionals

WOULD LIKE

1) She is not enjoying the party and would go home.

She is not enjoying the party and would like to go home.

Distinguish "she would go" ("[lei] andrebbe") from "she would like to go" ("[lei] vorrebbe andare"). See also 2) and 3) below.

2) In the future I would become a teacher.

In the future I would like to become a teacher.

3) When I have enough money, I would get married.

When I have enough money, I would like to get married.

"I would get married" means "Mi sposerei"; "vorrei sposarmi" is "I would like to get married".

1ST CONDITIONAL

4) If she will accept, I will be very happy.

If she accepts, I will be very happy.

See also 2) and 3) in the chapter Future Forms.

5) I will be with you by six o'clock unless the traffic isn't bad.

I will be with you by six o'clock unless the traffic is bad.

See also 7) in the chapter Conjunctions.

2ND CONDITIONAL

6) If I were in you, I wouldn't do that.

If I were you, I wouldn't do that.

7) If you wouldn't be a teacher, what did you do?

If you weren't a teacher, what would you do?

3RD CONDITIONAL

8) I would preferred to go abroad then.

I would have preferred to go abroad then.

9) If I would been alone, I had not done it.

If I had been alone, I would not have done it.

10) If I <u>had</u> the chance, I would have travelled round the world.

If I had had the chance, I would have travelled round the world.

INDIRECT/REPORTED SPEECH

11) We should wait for her. She said she <u>would have come</u>.

We should wait for her. She said she would come.

"Will" in direct speech/thought becomes "would" in reported speech/thought ("She said 'I will do it'" becomes "She said she would do it"). See also 12) to 15) below.

12) My parents were certain that sooner or later I <u>will</u> become a nun.

My parents were certain that sooner or later I would become a nun.

13) I thought it <u>should have been</u> difficult but it was not.

I thought it would be difficult but it was not.

14) I thought the film <u>would have been</u> better.

I thought the film would be better.

15) I was afraid that I <u>would never have seen</u> my family again.

I was afraid that I would never see my family again.

16) I wish the political system here changed.

I wish the political system here would change.

After "wish", use "would" to refer to a desire that something will happen in the future.

EXERCISES

A. Match each sentence beginning to a suitable ending:

1) When I finish university, I would...

2) You really should...

3) I was happy at that school and would...

4) She would like to get...

5) We were afraid that he...

6) I think I'd like...

7) If you had followed my advice, this...

8) My grandfather always said that it...

9) If I had had any idea what was going on, I...
10) I wish the...
11) Did you think it...
12) I know I shouldn't...

a) ...have been honest with me from the start.
b) ...would never happen.
c) ...like to become a journalist.
d) ...would be easier?
e) ...eat this kind of thing but it's so tempting!
f) ...married in a country church.
g) ...weather would improve.
h) ...would have done something about it.
i) ...have preferred not to move.
j) ...would never have happened.
k) ...to wait a little longer before making a final decision.
l) ...would not agree to the proposal.

B. Write answers to the following questions, then ask the questions to your study partner and make a note of his/her answers:
1) Where would you most like to live?
2) What will you do if you can't sleep tonight?
3) When you were a child, what job did you imagine you would do as an adult?
4) Where would you be if you weren't here now?
5) If you had had the chance to go to school in another country, which one would you have chosen?
6) What do you think politicians should do differently?

Transitive or Intransitive

1) I would like to <u>tell</u> about how football can be beneficial.

I would like to tell you about how football can be beneficial. / I would like to talk about how football can be beneficial.

"Tell" is occasionally used without any kind of object in idiomatic expressions ("She knows but she won't tell"; "Pray tell!") but in the vast majority of cases it requires one ("Sooner or later he will have to tell us"; "She never tells the truth").

2) I think it is better to <u>discuss face to face</u>.

I think it is better to discuss things face to face.

"Discuss" is not usually used without an explicit object. One exception to this is in essay instructions (e.g. "English food is better than Italian food. Discuss.").

3) This is why I prefer DVDs; if you go to the cinema, you have to <u>wear</u> and go out.

This is why I prefer DVDs; if you go to the cinema, you have to get dressed and go out.

The verb "wear", in the sense of "indossare", is transitive and therefore requires an object ("She never wears trousers"; "What are you wearing to the party tomorrow?"); it never translates "vestirsi".

4) She prefers to <u>dress casual clothes</u>.

She prefers to wear casual clothes. / She prefers to dress casual/casually.

The verb "dress" is not used transitively with clothing. It may, however, be used with a person as its object (e.g. "It takes her ages to dress the baby"; "He can't dress himself any more").

5) At the end of summer I decided to <u>dismiss</u> and look for a new job.

At the end of summer I decided to quit/resign and look for a new job.

"Dismiss", like the more informal verbs "fire" and "sack", is transitive and means "licenziare"; it is often used in the passive ("He was dismissed for persistent lateness"). To translate "licenziarsi", use "resign" (formal) or "quit" (informal).

6) He is <u>living</u> a difficult moment.

He is having a difficult time. / He is going through a difficult time.

Avoid using the verb "live" with an object except in idiomatic expressions such as "living the life of Riley" or "living the dream". See also 7) below.

7) Everybody <u>lives</u> this kind of situation.

Everybody experiences this kind of situation.

8) That's why I have <u>experimented some ways</u> to relax.

That's why I have experimented with some ways to relax.

9) This <u>allows to</u> recharge the battery anywhere.

This allows you to recharge the battery anywhere. / This makes it possible to recharge the battery anywhere.

The verb "allow" is rarely used intransitively. One exception is with the word "time" as a subject ("We'll do it if time allows").

10) It <u>encourages to</u> be positive.

It encourages people to be positive. / It encourages positivity

The verb "encourage" is rarely used intransitively.

11) I <u>dreamed</u> their wedding last night.

I dreamed about their wedding last night.

12) I suggest you to visit the old town and the castle.

I suggest (that) you visit the old town and the castle.

Similarly: "I recommend (that) you visit the old town and the castle". Contrast with: "I advise you to visit the old town and the castle".

13) My interest in music <u>renewed</u> at school.

My interest in music was renewed/revived/rekindled at school.

The verb "renew" is not used intransitively.

14) He <u>orders to do it</u> immediately.

He orders it to be done immediately. / He orders him/her/them to do it immediately.

EXERCISES

A. Match each sentence beginning to a suitable ending:

1) He is living...

2) The built-in flash allows...

3) They dismissed...

4) Last night I dreamed...

5) She prefers to wear...

6) There's an emergency meeting to discuss...

7) She quit...

8) This kind of initiative encourages...

9) We are having...

10) They always dress...

11) We have been experimenting...

12) Caesar ordered...

a) ...a difficult time.

b) ...casual clothes.

c) ...him for inappropriate behaviour.

d) ...it to be done that same day.

e) ...the proposed strike action.

f) ...people to use their cars less.

g) ...after they increased the working hours.

h) ...the baby in blue.

i) ...about the demonstration.

j) ...with different kinds of food.

k) ...you to use the camera even in poor lighting.

l) ...the life of Riley.

B. Write answers to the following questions, then ask the questions to your study partner and make a note of his/her answers:

1) What did you dream about last night?

2) Which Italian specialities do you suggest foreign visitors try first?

3) What kind of clothes do you wear around the house?

4) Have you experienced any difficult situations recently?

5) What can you tell me about the place you were born?

6) What kinds of things should schools not allow students to do?

Word Order

SEPARATING VERB & OBJECT

1) I enjoyed a lot secondary school.
I enjoyed secondary school a lot.

2) She likes very much this painting.
She likes this painting very much. / She very much likes this painting.

3) I like too much my job to change it.
I like my job too much to change it.

4) He tried again the exam the following year.
He tried the exam again the following year.

5) I have sold on commission four paintings this year.
I have sold four paintings on commission this year.

6) He obtains finally inner peace.
He finally obtains inner peace.

7) He changes very slowly his behaviour.
He changes his behaviour very slowly. / He very slowly changes his behaviour.

8) She wants to know better herself.
She wants to know herself better.

9) They spend together the rest of their lives.
They spend the rest of their lives together.

10) I remember still the expression on your face.
I still remember the expression on your face.

11) I hope to finish soon my studies.
I hope to finish my studies soon.

12) We haven't met here many helpful people.
We haven't met many helpful people here.

13) If I could, I would buy immediately another one.
If I could, I would buy another one immediately.

14) My sister got for her birthday the third book of the saga Harry Potter.
My sister got the third book of the Harry Potter saga for her birthday.

15) I was in second grade when I visited for the first time the museum.
I was in second grade when I visited the museum for the first time. / I was in second grade when I first visited the museum.

USING INTERROGATIVE FORM WHERE NOT REQUIRED
16) I know what is it.
I know what it is.
This is not a question: there is no reason to invert subject and verb.

17) Do you understand what are the problems?
Do you understand what the problems are?
The interrogative part of the question is "Do you understand...".

DIRECT OBJECT NEEDED IN ENGLISH
18) He doesn't allow to drive it to anyone.
He doesn't allow anyone to drive it.

19) I taught to play guitar at the kids.
I taught the kids to play the guitar.

MISPLACED ADJECTIVES
20) I would like to know how the English class is big.
I would like to know how big the English class is.

21) I will become a journalist rich and famous.
I will become a rich and famous journalist.

22) It is a difficulty apparently insuperable.
It is an apparently insuperable difficulty.

23) There are other three reasons.
There are three other reasons.

24) I live in Alberobello, a pretty town famous for old, beautiful buildings.

I live in Alberobello, a pretty town famous for beautiful old buildings.

25) I love your new cut hair.

I love your new haircut.

26) He is a character very strange and sometimes ridiculous.

He is a very strange and sometimes ridiculous character. / He is a very strange, sometimes ridiculous character.

INVERSION OF SUBJECT & VERB

27) Then was born my brother Marco.

Then my brother Marco was born.

28) I eat precooked food that prepares my mum.

I eat precooked food that my mum prepares.

29) I don't know if exists Heaven.

I don't know if Heaven exists.

30) I think is worth watching this film.

I think this film is worth watching. / I think it is worth watching this film.

31) Remarkable is the direction of Paolo Sorrentino.

Paolo Sorrentino's direction is remarkable. / The direction, by Paolo Sorrentino, is remarkable.

32) Today in many countries is still banned the film.

Today in many countries the film is still banned. / Today the film is still banned in many countries. / The film is still banned in many countries today.

MISPLACING OBJECT WITH PHRASAL VERBS

33) They <u>brought up him</u> like a son.

They brought him up like a son.

Note that with "bring up" and many other phrasal verbs, the position of the object pronoun is fixed while the position of the object noun is flexible: "They brought up the boy like a son" / "They brought the boy up like a son". See also 34) below and 7) in the chapter Phrasal Verbs.

34) I love chocolate too much. I could never <u>give up it</u>.

I love chocolate too much. I could never give it up.

But, as in the previous example, the position of the object noun is flexible: "I could never give chocolate up" / "I could never give up chocolate."

OTHER

35) I and my class with my English teacher went to Malta.

I went to Malta with my English teacher and my class.

36) I have lived since I was born in Barletta.

I have lived in Barletta since I was born.

37) There was nothing that disliked me about it.

There was nothing that I disliked about it.

See also 1) in the chapter Different Language, Different Structure.

38) They were friends who I thought there would be for ever.

They were friends who I thought would be there for ever.

39) If the teachers there aren't, the students don't study.

If the teachers aren't there, the students don't study.

40) It was a quite big house.

It was quite a big house.

41) I didn't expect a so difficult question.

I didn't expect such a difficult question.

42) When I was a child I liked to play tennis table.

When I was a child I liked to play table tennis.

43) Only after the war the importance of the movie was understood.

Only after the war was the importance of the movie understood.

44) Not only I enjoyed it, I loved it.

Not only did I enjoy it, I loved it.

45) Only by looking at them, you can understand what they are thinking.

Only by looking at them, can you understand what they are thinking.

46) Have a good day you too!
You have a good day too!

47) I love watching series TV.
I love watching TV series.

EXERCISES

A. Complete the sentences by inserting the word provided into the most appropriate position:

1) I have three cousins in Basilicata. (OTHER)
2) Have a great holiday too! (YOU)
3) She would like to get to know her in-laws. (BETTER)
4) Do you know where are? (THEY)
5) It would be great to spend a couple of weeks. (TOGETHER)
6) Do you remember how the portions were in that restaurant? (SMALL)
7) Only when the dish is almost ready, you add the cheese on top. (SHOULD)
8) We are going to begin the renovation work. (SOON)
9) I had never seen a dilapidated building. (SUCH)
10) She's the one person who I know will always be for me. (THERE)
11) Try that number. (AGAIN)
12) You should contact your nearest police station. (IMMEDIATELY)

B. Reorder the words to form complete sentences:

1) enjoyed / much / holiday / we / very / the
2) to / the / teaching / my / play / is / piano / me / sister
3) slowly / are / facade / the / they / restoring
4) touch / anyone / allow / she / it / doesn't / to
5) certainly / reading / worth / is / book / the
6) frightening / a / was / experience / quite / it
7) with / occasion / the / remember / pleasure / we
8) first / snow / the / remember / I / for / saw / time / I / when
9) it / much / to / he / it / up / too / give / likes
10) birthday / her / beautiful / for / new / got / pair / of / she / a / earrings

C. Write answers to the following questions, then ask the questions to your study partner and make a note of his/her answers:

1) How much do you enjoy studying English?

2) What did you get for your last birthday?

3) If you had a Ferrari, who would you allow to drive it?

4) What's your favourite TV series?

5) How did the students behave in the classroom at your school when the teachers weren't there?

6) Which recent Italian films are most worth watching?

7) Do you think Heaven exists?

8) When was your youngest relative born?

9) How old were you when you first rode a bicycle?

10) What do you think of my haircut?

Wrong Word

1) It will be the <u>journey</u> of our dreams.

It will be the holiday of our dreams.

"Journey" conveys the idea of travel between two points. It does not include the time spent at your destination. See also 4) in the chapter Countable or Uncountable and 2) below.

2) During the <u>travel</u> to New York they get to know each other.

During the journey to New York they get to know each other.

See also 4) in the chapter Countable or Uncountable.

3) I <u>knew</u> my boyfriend on a train.

I met my boyfriend on a train.

4) Did you manage to <u>know</u> what time the film starts?

Did you manage to find out what time the film starts?

When "sapere" is used in the sense of "scoprire", it is usually translated with "find out" or "discover" ("When his girlfriend discovered/found out what he had done, she broke up with him").

5) Can you <u>smash</u> the potatoes while I set the table?

Can you mash the potatoes while I set the table?

See also 2) in the chapter Almost.

6) When I was twelve, <u>all</u> changed.

When I was twelve, everything changed.

It is more usual to translate the Italian pronoun "tutto" with "everything" than with "all", although there are exceptions to this ("All you need is love").

7) I started to travel by public transport as my high school was in another <u>country</u>.

I started to travel by public transport as my high school was in another town.

"Country" translates "paese" in the sense of "nazione".

8) It tells the <u>history</u> of two young people in 1940.

It tells the story of two young people in 1940.

A "history" is an attempt to provide a factual account or record of the past; it is also the name of the subject ("storia") studied at school and university. Fictional narratives are "stories". See also 9) below.

9) It is a romantic <u>history</u>.

It is a romantic story.

10) I was really in love with him but now our <u>history</u> is over.

I was really in love with him but now our relationship is over.

11) I discovered my husband <u>had a story</u> with another woman.

I discovered my husband was having an affair with another woman.

The word "affair" in the sense intended here often suggests disapproval on the part of the speaker. A more neutral sense can be conveyed by "relationship", as in 10) above.

12) She decided to become a <u>nursery</u>.

She decided to become a nurse.

A nursery is a place where very young children are looked after ("asilo" or "nido") or where young plants and trees are grown ("vivaio").

13) I can't make plans because there are few working <u>occasions</u>.

I can't make plans because there are few work/job opportunities.

"Occasion" has a narrower range of meaning than its Italian equivalent.

14) He is <u>trying</u> an excuse not to sell the house.

He is looking for an excuse not to sell the house.

"Try" can translate "cercare" in the sense of "tentare" ("We are trying to learn English") but it is not used in the sense intended here.

15) She was <u>constricted</u> by her father to marry a nobleman.

She was obliged by her father to marry a nobleman.

"Constricted" means narrowed ("constricted blood vessels") or restricted ("constricted breathing").

16) If you are <u>animated</u> by a sense of duty and love, you can do anything.

If you are motivated/inspired/driven by a sense of duty and love, you can do anything.

17) My childhood was <u>animated</u>.

My childhood was lively.

We often use "animated" to describe a person who is talking or gesturing excitedly ("She gets very animated when she is discussing her work") or a lively conversation.

18) I'm a good <u>cooker</u>.
I'm a good cook.
A "cooker" is a domestic appliance, not a person.

19) He <u>accepts</u> to do it.
He agrees to do it.
"Accept" is never followed by an infinitive.

20) When I finish university, I want to <u>reach</u> my fiancé in Milan.
When I finish university, I want to join my fiancé in Milan.
"To reach" is sometimes used with a person as its object in the sense of to succeed in contacting [e.g. by telephone] ("I've been trying all morning but I haven't been able to reach him") but not in the sense of "to go to".

21) The trains <u>reach</u> only the main cities.
The trains only serve the main cities.

22) At seventeen I <u>entered in</u> a punk band.
At seventeen I joined a punk band.

23) I believe in the <u>worth</u> of art.
I believe in the value of art.

24) In June I <u>overcame</u> an audition.
In June I succeeded in an audition. / In June I passed an audition.

25) No one can <u>overpass</u> his genius.
No one can surpass his genius.

26) Philosophy is a subject that <u>charms</u> me.
Philosophy is a subject that fascinates me.

27) My father is a <u>blacksmith</u> and he works in a small factory.
My father is a metalworker and he works in a small factory.
The term "blacksmith" is usually used in historical contexts and is often associated with the making of horseshoes.

28) It has a big, <u>coloured</u> market.
It has a big, colourful market.

29) My school gave me a good <u>preparation</u>.
My school gave me a good education.

30) Speaking is an art that few possess; it <u>needs</u> charisma.
Speaking is an art that few possess; it requires charisma.

31) She gets divorced because of her husband's <u>treason</u>.
She gets divorced because of her husband's betrayal.
"Treason" is a political crime, a betrayal of the state.

32) Sunday is the day when we all <u>stay</u> together.
Sunday is the day when we are all together / we all spend time together / we all get together.
The Italian verb "stare" is hardly ever translated with "stay". See also 33) below and 8) in the chapter Classics.

33) At university I <u>stay</u> a lot of time with my new friends.
At university I spend a lot of time with my new friends.
See also 8) in the chapter Classics.

34) I hope to <u>spend</u> a good day!
I hope to have a good day.

35) Chaplin <u>interprets</u> two roles in this film.
Chaplin plays two roles in this film.
See also 36) below.

36) I liked the <u>interpretations</u> of Jude Law and Natalie Portman.
I liked the performances of Jude Law and Natalie Portman.

37) I loved classical <u>matters</u> at school.
I loved classical subjects at school.
See also 27) in the chapter False Friends.

38) All of the characters in the book are <u>well-built</u>.
All of the characters in the book are well-constructed.
"Well-built" means physically robust.

39) I hope I will be able to <u>realise</u> my objectives.
I hope I will be able to achieve my objectives.

40) You need <u>fantasy</u> to be a good writer.
You need imagination to be a good writer.

41) The nearest bank is on the next <u>island</u>, just past the traffic lights.
The nearest bank is on the next block, just past the traffic lights.

42) The maths teacher's <u>expositions</u> were very difficult to understand.
The maths teacher's explanations were very difficult to understand.
See also 19) in the chapter False Friends.

43) I start work in <u>half</u> September.
I start work in mid-September.

44) I really enjoyed this film. I will <u>suggest</u> it to my friends.
I really enjoyed this film. I will recommend it to my friends.

45) She meets him in a Manhattan <u>coffee</u>.
She meets him in a Manhattan coffee bar / coffee shop / café.

46) What do the other <u>components</u> of your family say?
What do the other members of your family say?
Avoid using "component" to refer to a human being or other living creature.

47) I <u>attend</u> the first year of university.
I am in the first year of university.

48) I did a theatre course and acted in my first <u>representation</u>.
I did a theatre course and acted in my first play.

49) He <u>greets</u> everybody and he goes off.
He says goodbye to everybody and he goes off.
In spoken English the Italian term "salutare" is usually translated with "say hello [to...]" (when you meet someone) and "say goodbye [to...]" (when you take leave of someone). "Greet" is a rather formal equivalent of "say hello to...".

50) I saw my parents only in the morning when they <u>carried</u> me to school.

I saw my parents only in the morning when they took me to school.

"Carried me" means "mi portavano in braccio".

51) At nineteen I <u>matriculated to</u> the Faculty of Arts at the University of Bari.

At nineteen I enrolled at the Faculty of Arts at the University of Bari.

Although the term "matriculate" exists in the sense of "enrol", it is rarely used outside of formal administrative contexts.

52) I have great memories of Barcelona and I hope to <u>come</u> back there in the future.

I have great memories of Barcelona and I hope to go back there in the future.

You can use "come" to describe movement towards the current position of the speaker and/or his/her interlocutor(s). For movement away from the current position of the speaker and/or his/her interlocutor(s), use "go". See also 2) in the chapter Phrasal Verbs.

53) I have a very large stereo because I love to <u>hear</u> music.

I have a very large stereo because I love to listen to music.

You "hear" any sounds that reach your ears ("She heard a noise in the other room"; "Even though we have double-glazing, we can still hear the traffic"); you listen as the result of a deliberate choice ("Why do you never listen to what I say?").

54) This film <u>remembers</u> me my adolescence.

This film reminds me of my adolescence.

55) We are <u>waiting</u> for them late tomorrow evening.

We are expecting them late tomorrow evening.

56) The Vatican tried to <u>avoid</u> the distribution of the film in Italy.

The Vatican tried to prevent the distribution of the film in Italy.

57) Every day I have to <u>move</u> to Bari.

Every day I have to travel/commute to Bari.

When used with the name of a place as its object, the verb "to move to" means "trasferirsi a". See also 58) below.

58) When I was seven years old, my family <u>transferred</u> to Turin.

When I was seven years old, my family moved to Turin.

59) I like to know about the historical events that <u>signed</u> the past.
I like to know about the historical events that shaped the past.

60) I've learned to think outside the <u>lines</u> and find innovative solutions to problems.
I've learned to think outside the box and find innovative solutions to problems.

61) I was born in Carbonara, a <u>hamlet</u> of Bari.
I was born in Carbonara, a suburb of Bari.
A "hamlet" is a rural settlement, usually smaller than a village and not governed by a municipal body of its own.

62) Looking at this photo, I <u>try</u> the same feeling.
Looking at this photo, I get/have the same feeling.

63) From the boat you can see the town from a different <u>point of view</u>.
From the boat you can see the town from a different vantage point / perspective.
The expression "point of view" is usually used in the sense of opinion ("I'd like to hear your point of view on this").

64) In cities with serious traffic problems, motorcycles are more <u>comfortable</u> than cars.
In cities with serious traffic problems, motorcycles are more convenient than cars.
"Comfortable" describes something which enhances physical well-being ("a comfortable mattress"; "a comfortable armchair"; etc); "convenient" translates "comodo" in the sense of easy to use or practical.

65) The problem is that many companies do not <u>respect</u> these laws.
The problem is that many companies do not comply with these laws.

66) We left the car in a <u>parking</u> at the airport.
We left the car in a car park at the airport.
"Parking" is an action, not a place ("Parking is always difficult in this part of town"). Note that if you are referring to a place for a single car, the correct term is "parking space". See also 18 in the chapter Classics.

67) The archaeological <u>exposition</u> was fascinating.
The archaeological exhibition was fascinating.

EXERCISES

A. For each pair of options in italics, underline the more suitable term:

1) She always wears very *colourful/coloured* clothes.

2) The book tells the *story/history* of a man who is obsessed with the *story/history* of 20th century Germany.

3) The *travel/journey* from the airport to the hotel was a nightmare but apart from that it was a great *travel/trip*.

4) I first *knew/met* him at church and he struck me as very honest but then I *knew/found out* from his ex-wife that he had had a number of *affairs/stories* behind her back.

5) My husband loves living in Cambridge and I don't think he would *accept/agree* to *move/transfer* to a smaller *country/town*.

6) I studied science *subjects/matters* at school but I've forgotten *everything/all*.

7) We had a *café/coffee* in a *café/coffee* a couple of *blocks/islands* away from the railway station.

8) He's a great *cook/cooker*: even his *mashed/smashed* potatoes taste like heaven.

9) She is *looking for/trying* an excuse not to tell the other *components/members* of her family about it.

10) I'll *join/reach* you in Paris on Wednesday and then *carry/take* you on to London with me at the weekend.

11) It's the kind of work that *wants/requires imagination/fantasy* and an ability to think outside the *box/lines*.

12) The characters in the film are all *well-built/well-constructed* and the *performances/interpretations* by the two leading actors are magnificent.

B. Rearrange the letters provided to form a suitable word to fill each gap:

1) He had the _____ to go and work in San Francisco but he turned it down. (TIPONORYTUP)

2) These schools provide students with an excellent _____ . (UNOTEADIC)

3) I haven't yet _____ all my objectives. (HAVIDECE)

4) Her _____ of how it works couldn't have been clearer. (ATALPINNOXE)

5) He is still trying to come to terms with his wife's _____ . (ABLARETY)

6) The idea is to _____ smugglers bringing drugs into the country. (TEVRNPE)

172

7) They were _____ by circumstances to sell up and move. (GIDOLEB)

8) She retired from public life and is now living in a quiet _____ of Milan. (RUBBUS)

9) Is it a method you would _____ to other students? (MEMODRENC)

10) These events undoubtedly played a part in _____ his personality. (GISPHAN)

C. Write answers to the following questions, then ask the questions to your study partner and make a note of his/her answers:

1) How many times have you moved house?

2) What are the things that remind you of your childhood?

3) Of all the places you have visited, which one would you most like to go back to?

4) Have you ever had to commute?

5) How well do the other members of your family speak English?

6) Have you ever acted in a play?

7) Which of your long-term objectives are you most anxious to achieve?

8) How often do you get together with your family?

9) What were your favourite subjects at school?

10) Have you been obliged recently to do anything you didn't want to?

You Might Want to Rephrase That!

1) My father is 48 years old. My mother is older than him; she is 51 years older.
My father is 48 years old. My mother is older than him; she is 51 years old.
If the mother were really "51 years older", she would be 99.

2) Other skills: good at hand jobs.
Other skills: good at manual tasks.
Certain abilities are perhaps best not mentioned on your CV.

3) Dear teacher, I want your issue.
Dear teacher, please could you send me the course materials.
In formal legal English, "issue" means "children".

4) I had to stop milking the baby so I could go back to work.
I had to stop breastfeeding the baby so I could go back to work.
You milk a cow!

5) I'm going to become an artistic manageress.
I'm going to become a manageress in the arts sector.

6) Sanitary areas are my passion.
I'm extremely interested in the medical field.

7) We were never together because we wanted it at different times.
We were never together because we were never interested in each other at the same time.
Only ever "wanting it" at different times is probably a good reason not to start a relationship but this is not what the speaker intended here.

8) My mother was working as a pastry in a famous cake shop in Ruvo.
My mother was working as a pastry cook / as a patissier in a famous cake shop in Ruvo.
A "pastry" is something you eat, not a person.

9) Thank you for inviting us. Where can we leave our clothes?
Thank you for inviting us. Where can we leave our coats?
Although grammatically correct, the question "Where can we leave our clothes?" may alarm your hosts.

10) Stop greasing your teeth!

Stop gritting your teeth!

"To grease" means "ungere" or "lubrificare".

11) My father works as a dealer in a clothing store.

My father works as a salesman / shop assistant in a clothing store.

The term "dealer" is used to describe very specific types of work ("car dealer"; "financial dealer"; "antique[s] dealer"; "art dealer"; etc). In other contexts it risks being interpreted as an abbreviation of "drug dealer".

12) He has got black eyes and brown hair.

He has got dark eyes and brown hair.

A "black eye" is usually the result of bruising ("lividi") caused by a blow to the area around the eye.

13) I liked Mr Rochester's figure.

I liked the figure of Mr Rochester.

"Mr Rochester's figure" is his physical shape. Opinions regarding its attractiveness are unlikely to impress a teacher or examiner reading an essay on "Jane Eyre".

14) I am tied a lot to the animals: I love cats and dogs.

I am very fond of animals: I love cats and dogs.

Expressing your love of animals by binding yourself to them with a rope or cord is, of course, theoretically possible, but to be discouraged.

15) One day I found a cat near my grandfather's house. It was small and chilled.

One day I found a cat near my grandfather's house. It was small and very cold / freezing cold.

In contemporary English, "chilled" is used to describe either food that has been refrigerated prior to eating ("Serve chilled, with fresh cream") or, informally, a person who is extremely relaxed.

16) I have a cold. I don't smell.

I have a cold. I can't smell anything.

"I don't smell" means "non puzzo". See also 4) and 5) in the chapter Tenses - Present.

17) I need to be convicted before I go to work in England.

I need to be convinced before I go to work in England.

"To be convicted" is to be found formally guilty of a crime ("He was convicted of murder").

18) It's not easy to paint without a weasel.

It's not easy to paint without an easel.

"Weasel" means "donnola". Most artists manage fine without one.

PART 2: ANSWER KEYS

Classics

A.

1) He **was** born in London.

2) In my family **there are** five people.

3) When I finish school I'd like to **be a** teacher.

4) I'm **doing** a master's.

5) I suggest **they ask** an expert.

6) I have **a degree** in engineering.

7) Thank you **for everything**!

8) Where did you and your girlfriend **meet**?

9) He is on the phone **at the moment**.

10) We spent our holiday at a **camp-site**.

11) The holiday was great but the food was **nothing special**.

B. Sample Answers

1) I was born in Bari in the south-east of Italy.

2) There are five people in my family. / There are five of us.

3) I would most like to be a professional footballer.

4) My favourite camp-site is in a wood near a beach on the Salento coast.

5) Being without my phone wouldn't be a huge problem for me.

6) By train. / By bus. / I drive. / On foot.

7) We were at school together. / We met at a yoga course.

8) I suggest foreign tourists visit Rome and Florence first.

9) I did a six-month training course before I started my current job.

Adjectives

A.

1) She has a siesta **every** afternoon from three till four.

2) He isn't pretentious at all! He's the most **down-to-earth** person you could wish to meet.

3) My wife is working that day so we wouldn't be able to go to the wedding in **any** case.

4) I don't like the place: it's full of souvenir shops and too **touristy**!

5) It was invented in the **early** twentieth century.

6) Although it is five hundred years old, the story is still **relevant** today.

7) Gaudi's architecture is extremely **unusual**.

8) The hotel has a very **distinctive** style.

9) This is an **excellent** example of late Impressionist art.

10) You should try it! It's a **fun** way to learn.

11) I love this music: it's really **haunting**.

12) It's very difficult to see an end to the current **economic** crisis.

B. Sample Answers

1) I drink coffee and go running every morning.

2) It's very touristy. / It's quite touristy. / It's not touristy at all.

3) The most distinctive building in our town is the castle.

4) I can never remember jokes, even the funny ones.

5) Some of Morricone's music is very haunting.

6) I practically never listen to classical music.

7) I'd say I'm pretty optimistic.

8) I think I'd describe my younger brother as quiet.

9) I'm always having unusual experiences!

10) My best friend is very down-to-earth.

Adverbs

A.

1) We spent **almost** all the money we had.

2) Parachuting is **very** dangerous.

3) Matera is **absolutely** unique.

4) The film has been **much** talked about.

5) We're going to go out for a walk **even** if it rains.

6) – Did you enjoy the holiday?   – **Very** much!

7) You really should read this article. It's **extremely** interesting!

8) Everything went **well**.

9) We have **always** lived in this house.

10) It cost me, or **rather** my father, a lot of money.

Almost

A.

1) **Women** are generally better than men at this kind of thing.

2) Do you prefer roast potatoes or **mashed**?

3) What are her **plans** for the future?

4) There are eight major **planets** in the solar system.

5) He **fell** off his bike while he was riding to school.

6) Everyone else was laughing but I didn't think it was **funny**.

7) The end doesn't always justify the **means**.

8) She **joined** the Communist party when she was a student.

9) There is no **heroine** to compare with Elizabeth Bennet.

10) Unfortunately the hotel didn't have a swimming **pool**.

11) I feel better **than** before.

B. Sample Answers

1) I saw a very funny Benigni film on TV the other day.

2) For the moment I don't have any plans for the weekend.

3) I must have been about seven when I first fell in love.

4) Happy endings aren't very important for me.

5) I often get stuck in the traffic at rush hour.

6) I don't think there are any political parties worth joining.

7) I think the idea that the end justifies the means is very dangerous.

Class-shifting

A.

1) You can pay on **arrival** or when you leave.

2) I am **truly** sorry about what happened.

3) They say that **Jewish** and Italian mothers have a lot in common.

4) I never feel at **ease** in the company of people like that.

5) It was a very difficult **choice** to make.

6) The judges' decision was highly **controversial**.

7) A number of **volunteers** helped the local people to clear up after the flooding.

8) They have been travelling around **southern** Italy for several weeks.

B. Sample Answers

1) I was once in charge of a group of students on a study holiday in London.

2) I'm fairly satisfied with most of my choices.

3) My relatives live all over the place.

4) I used to work as a volunteer for the Red Cross.

5) Ten! I'm very argumentative.

6) I think what I will remember most about my adolescence is the school trips.

7) My train is often cancelled or delayed because of "unforeseen circumstances".

Collocations

A.

1) We were introduced by a **mutual** friend.

2) Estate agents **earn** a lot more money than teachers.

3) At the beginning of the 20th century Maria Montessori introduced a new educational **approach**.

4) What kind of results do you hope to **achieve**?

5) We **had** some great times together.

6) It's a beautiful building but it needs **renovating**.

7) She has a **great** passion for art.

8) What kind of school did you **go to**?

9) Because of his **financial** problems, my brother has had to take on a second job.

10) I prefer films with happy **endings**.

11) Learning a foreign language is an excellent way to **broaden** your cultural **horizons**.

12) We had a wonderful, **carefree** childhood.

B. Sample Answers

1) I went to primary school in Rome, where I grew up.

2) It was renovated last year. / No it hasn't but it certainly needs renovating!

3) I only weigh the ingredients if I'm cooking something special.

4) The ending of "100 Years of Solitude" really surprised me.

5) My greatest passion is sculpture.

6) The best ways to broaden your cultural horizons are reading and travelling.

7) I try to expand my English vocabulary by reading as much as I can and keeping a notebook.

Comparatives & Superlatives
A.

1) c) Which of the two holidays **was more fun?**

2) i) We'll need at **least another five hundred grams.**

3) k) My cold is getting **worse and worse.**

4) h) Out of all these problems, unemployment is the **worst.**

5) a) There was less **traffic than I expected.**

6) l) Money is not as **important as some people seem to believe.**

7) j) Which of the two jokes **did you think was funnier?**

8) e) It is more **useful than you might think.**

9) b) There were fewer **people than last time.**

10) g) These days he spends **most of his time gardening.**

11) d) The problem is the same **as before.**

12) f) It is much **nearer than the other supermarket.**

B.

1) It is more interesting **than** the other one.

2) Just try to do your **best**.

3) Where in the world would you **most** like to live?.

4) It will cost at **least** €50.

5) Who is the brightest student **in** the class?

6) Mine is the same **as** yours.

7) Lecce is not as big **as** Naples.

8) They live in the **northernmost** part of Scotland.

C. Sample Answers

1) As far as I'm concerned, pretty much everything is more fun than shopping.

2) I live much nearer to the mountains than to the sea.

3) I think (and hope) it's getting better.

4) I most dislike rudeness. / I dislike rudeness most. / What I most dislike is rudeness.

5) The hardest thing about English is understanding when people speak fast.

6) In my opinion, the most interesting town in our region is Matera.

7) I spend most of my money on clothes and shoes.

Conjunctions

A.

1) He quit his job **because** he couldn't live on such a low salary.

2) I'll take my credit card **in case** they don't accept cash.

3) **Although** the sea was quite rough, there were people swimming off the local beach.

4) For their honeymoon they are undecided between Japan **and** New Zealand.

5) Their electricity will be cut off **unless** they pay the bill by tomorrow.

6) We can't decide **whether** to go or not.

7) She doesn't speak the language **even though** she has been living there for years.

8) They wouldn't be able to afford that house **even if** they won the lottery.

9) I'll love you **until** I die and I hope you'll love me **as long as** you live!

10) Those on the left are pushing for better services **while** those on the right want lower taxes.

11) He just went ahead and did it **in spite of the fact** I had warned him not to.

B. Sample Answers

1) Whether I have a dessert or not depends on how full I am.

2) I eat lettuce when I'm on a diet even though I don't really like it.

3) I would accept the offer of my ideal job even if it meant moving to Timbuktu!

4) I can't study very well while I'm listening to music.

5) I will remember my first kiss and my graduation day as long as I live.

Countable and Uncountable Nouns

A.

1) This one is definitely my favourite Neruda **_poem_**.

2) Do you prefer prose or **_poetry_**?

3) She's extremely interested in **_photography_**.

4) I love that **_photograph_** of you holding the baby.

5) We have a lot of **_work_** to do today.

6) My friend Margherita has found a **_job_** with a company in Sweden.

7) How was your **_trip_** to San Francisco?

8) They say that **_travel_** broadens the mind.

9) How far is it to the nearest **_beach_**?

10) I'm going to have my **_hair_** cut this afternoon.

B. Sample Answers

1) I have had all kinds of jobs.

2) I last had my hair cut a couple of weeks ago.

3) The nearest beach to where I live is about forty minutes drive away.

4) I once wrote a love poem when I was a teenager.

5) It's a twenty-minute journey to school/university/work from where I live.

6) I devote more time to my homework but I sometimes help my mother with the housework.

7) If I could keep only one photograph, I would keep the one with my whole family in the garden.

8) The people I most often ask for advice are my older sister and my grandfather.

9) I'm spending as much time as I can but not as much as I should studying English.

Definite Article

A.

1) We often go walking in **_the_** countryside or in **_the_** mountains.

2) My brother supports ~~the~~ Juventus but I support ~~the~~ Inter.

3) Mum's cooking in **_the_** kitchen and Dad's working in **_the_** garden.

4) They came by ~~the~~ bus but they're going back on **_the_** train.

5) In ~~the~~ recent years he has been working less.

6) I loved ~~the~~ primary school, hated ~~the~~ secondary school and quite like ~~the~~ university.

7) I read somewhere that ~~the~~ 55% of children in ~~the~~ Europe watch ~~the~~ cartoons every day.

8) Vandals set fire to **the** secondary school opposite our house ~~the~~ last week.

9) I imagine that ~~the~~ life in ~~the~~ 16th century London was very different from today.

10) ~~The~~ Lucy's picture was in **the** newspaper ~~the~~ last month.

B. Sample Answers

1) Life's pretty good at the moment.

2) I have always preferred the mountains to the sea.

3) I turned 21 in 2013.

4) I spend much more time in the kitchen (than in the bathroom).

5) I've only been to two countries in Europe.

6) I speak Spanish and a little Chinese.

7) I preferred primary school to secondary school.

8) I spend about 20% of my waking hours studying.

9) I have been working extremely hard in recent weeks.

Different Language, Different Structure

A.

1) **That's [the reason] why** she will never do it.

2) Are there any good films **on** this week?

3) Your concentration must always be **as great as possible**.

4) He passed **his driving test**.

5) **It has got to the point where** I don't believe anything Italian politicians say.

6) **I have recently** started a yoga course.

7) He has lost the only **thing he had to live for**.

8) You **don't have to** answer.

9) We have similar tastes and a similar **idea of what it means to be a** couple.

10) You risk **finding yourself back at square one**.

11) One of them **has the same name as** my father.

12) I would like to **be well remembered**.

B. Sample Answers

1) I don't think there's anything good on this week. / There's an interesting film on at the multiplex.

2) Some of the paintings I saw in the Uffizi last year took my breath away.

3) To be honest, I don't feel I am very different from other people.

4) I passed my driving test when I was eighteen.

5) I tend to get angry very easily with certain people.

6) I got my nose pierced even though my father didn't want me to.

7) I suppose I'm a little afraid of the headmistress of our school.

Do & Make

A.

1) She **made** a serious mistake in marrying him.

2) Have you **done** your homework yet?

3) I can't find a job but I'm **doing** private lessons with some schoolchildren.

4) You need to **make** some changes to this before you submit it.

5) I have had to **make** a lot of sacrifices to be able to continue my studies.

6) It took three years to **do** the necessary research for this project.

7) I'll **make** you a cake for your birthday if you like.

8) When are you **doing** your next exam?

9) Did you **do** any sports when you were at school?

10) I didn't want to but the teacher **made** me rewrite it.

B.

1) My wife likes to **go** shopping with my credit card.

2) I've never **had** such a bad experience.

3) When she grows up she wants to **be** an engineer.

4) Did you **have** a nice holiday?

5) Could you **take** a photo of us, please?

6) I think I might **go for*** a walk along the seafront.

7) They decided to **have** a really big party to celebrate their engagement.

8) Changing my diet **helped** me get better.

9) We would like to **repeat** this experience.

10) He was able to **perform** some remarkable feats.

11) Can't you **get** your boss to buy you a new computer?

* "**have** a walk" and "**take** a walk" are also possible here

C. Sample Answers

1) I would like to have my own bedroom.

2) We take turns doing the shopping.

3) I very rarely go shopping for clothes.

4) The worst culinary experience I have ever had was in a tourist restaurant in Paris.

5) I last had a party when I graduated.

6) I prefer to take photos with my phone.

7) I make so many mistakes in English that it's difficult to say.

8) I haven't made as much progress as I would like since last year.

False Friends

A.

1) We have so many books we had to buy a new **bookcase**.

2) She is currently doing a **training course** in Milan.

3) Not passing the exam was an enormous **disappointment**.

4) I hope to have the **opportunity** to travel abroad.

5) We buy our fruit and vegetables from a local **farm**.

6) My sister is a **teacher** in a secondary school.

7) I studied economics and my dream is to start my own **business**.

8) His latest **novel** is about the Vietnam War.

9) I spent Christmas Day with about twenty of my **relatives**.

10) My **marks** in maths were never good.

11) I like school; history is the only **subject** I don't enjoy.

12) The road was blocked because of a bad car **accident**.

B.

1) This painting is a **real** masterpiece.

2) For many **opera** singers, performing at La Scala will only ever be a dream.

3) She never has anything interesting to say: I get **bored** just thinking about her!

4) You have to read it: it's **brilliant**!

5) The **current** economic crisis is much worse than the last one.

6) My colleague will now **explain** in more detail how the device works.

7) The only people left in the village now are **old** or middle-aged.

8) Thank you so much! It's really **kind** of you!

9) He is often **irritable** when he has had a hard day at work.

C. Sample Answers

1) I'd rather work in a library than in a bookshop.

2) I got my highest marks in maths and science.

3) I'd much prefer to own a farm.

4) I get nervous watching penalty shoot-outs.

5) Being tired or hungry makes me irritable.

6) I once won ten euros on a scratchcard.

7) The main disadvantage of living in an apartment building is being too close to other people.

8) The last novel I read was Dostoevsky's "Crime and Punishment".

9) The only disappointment I have had recently was not being able to go to the Bruce Springsteen concert.

Impersonal "it"
Sample answers

1) It takes me about two minutes to get dressed in the morning.

2) It is most important to remember the people who have been good to you.

3) In our family it is traditional to eat fish at Christmas.

4) Our relationship with our neighbours is very strained.

5) If you ask me, listening to English is more difficult than speaking it. / In my opinion, it is more difficult to listen to English than [to] speak it.

Indefinite Article
A.

1) My father is _____ retired now but he used to be *a* university professor.

2) She earns €7 *a* hour working as *a* hairdresser.

3) There were _____ lots of people and there was *a* lot of food.

4) I hope *one* day to see *a* UFO.

5) It's *an* honour to be invited to *a* house like this.

6) Being *an* only child is *an* unhappy experience for some.

7) She's _____ good company so I was happy to spend *a* few days with her.

8) _____ few people I know would not want to work for *a* company that treats its employees so well.

9) It's *a* useful gadget for *a* housewife to have.

10) My brother works in *a* gym four days *a* week.

11) Although there were _____ few opportunities for meeting people, from *one* day to the next I suddenly found myself with two new friends.

12) There are only *a* few biscuits left.

B. Sample Answers

1) The main disadvantage of being an only child is having nobody to play with.

2) I need to earn at least €1000 a month to get by.

3) I like to think I'm good company.

187

4) I wouldn't mind working for a company in the renewable energy sector.

5) I occasionally work as a waitress in a local pizzeria. / No, but I work as a barman sometimes.

6) The main advantages of being a pensioner are not having to get up so early and having plenty of free time.

Infinitive or -ing

A.

1) I don't like **being** so tall: it's always difficult **finding/to find** clothes that fit.

2) Where would you like **to sit**?

3) As a child, she always dreamed of **becoming** an architect.

4) I used to **play** a lot of football but I'm not used to **running** around any more.

5) That whole morning he never stopped **talking**, not even **to drink** his coffee.

6) I'm not inclined to **believe** anything that guy says.

7) **Bringing up** children is never an easy task.

8) He's determined to do it even if it means **getting up** at five a.m. every day.

9) All they ever do is **criticise**.

10) Are you looking forward to **spending** time with the in-laws?

11) Let's go back to **doing** it the way we did before.

12) Did you have any problems **parking** in the city centre?

13) I could spend hours **listening** to her **sing/singing** .

B. Sample Answers

1) I love the idea of **spending the day on the beach / not having to work / being able to fly**.

2) Where do you want **to meet / to put it / to pitch the tent**?

3) You have to avoid **spilling any of the liquid / bending this part / lifting heavy weights**.

4) She isn't prepared to risk **losing her job / catching his flu / not being there**.

5) He is afraid of **putting on weight / not passing the exam / being criticised**.

6) I hope to graduate and **move to Stockholm / start working immediately / find a good job**.

7) They didn't succeed in **convincing her / meeting the deadline / obtaining planning permission**.

8) Our plan is to **wait and see / invest heavily in human resources / switch to renewable energy**.

9) Always wash your hands before **eating / preparing food / inserting or removing your contact lenses**.

10) I don't have time **to do it / to waste on this / to deal with the problem now**.

11) The guidebook suggests **spending at least a day there / booking in advance / taking the longer route**.

12) They are undecided between **driving and taking the train / renting and buying / cooking and eating out**.

C. Sample Answers

1) I'm used to eating lots of pasta, vegetables and fruit.

2) As a child I used to eat pretty much everything except cheese.

3) My plans are to finish my exams and start looking for a job.

4) I dream of living in a house by the sea.

5) I usually avoid wearing a tie.

6) For me "relaxation" means lying on a beach and not having to think about work.

7) What I'm most looking forward to in the next few weeks is having a few days off.

Like & As

A.

1) **Like** most teenagers, he doesn't always see eye to eye with his parents.

2) She occasionally works **as** a waitress at weekends.

3) He wants to be an accountant, **like** his father.

4) Qualities such **as** reliability and thoroughness are essential for this job.

5) I admire him **as** a writer but I don't like him **as** a person.

6) He has always been **like** a brother to me.

7) Do you consider her _____ a friend?

8) I consider myself _____ a tolerant person.

9) It sounds **like** a wonderful place but it looks _____ expensive.

10) She looks **like** her mother.

11) He treats her **as** if she were his housekeeper.

12) Do you feel **like** going out this evening?

B. Sample Answers

1) Our Italian teacher encouraged us to think of her as a friend.

2) I most look like my father. / I don't look like anyone: I was adopted.

3) I feel like eating a whole bar of chocolate.

4) I would tell them where to go.

5) Life in London sounds expensive to me!

Missing Word

A.

1) When I was nine years **old**, my father bought me a fishing rod.

2) He wasn't able to go to the concert because **he** was sick.

3) Don't forget **to** turn off the gas before you go away.

4) A rescue team has been searching **for** the lost climbers for nearly two days now.

5) I haven't been able to go out much during the last **few** weeks.

6) What kind of music do you listen **to**?

7) If you hadn't been looking **at** that girl, you wouldn't have crashed the car!

8) We have two small children and for this **reason** it is difficult for us to go out in the evenings.

9) He is working together **with** his cousin.

10) Roberto Baggio played fifty-six times for the Italian national **team**.

11) They resolved the problem **by** calling in an expert.

12) We have decided against moving house: it's too **much** hassle.

B. Sample Answers

1) I forgot to reply to an important email yesterday.

2) I think Zola is the best player ever to have appeared for the Italian national team.

3) I avoided making my bed this morning because it was too much hassle.

4) I listen to all kinds of music except house.

5) Unfortunately, my life has hardly changed at all in the last few years.

Mistranslations

A.

1) Naples is big, noisy and chaotic. Siena, **on the other hand**, is small and quiet.

2) It's more a place for families and middle-aged couples than for **young people**.

3) Maths is one of my **strong points**.

4) This one is my favourite of all Conan Doyle's **detective stories**.

5) My **uncle and aunt** got married in 1995 and had their first child two years later.

6) I'd like to go to Spain or Greece or **in any case** somewhere hot.

7) If your mother needs a hand, we can **pop in** later this afternoon.

8) She had a bad day at work so she isn't **in a good mood**.

9) **As far as** my future **is concerned**, I would like to work in the field of publishing.

10) This job **gave me the opportunity** to travel.

11) **Be careful of** the ice on the mountain roads.

12) I'm sorry but I couldn't call you because I **had no signal on my phone**.

B. Sample Answers

1) I have three uncles and two aunts.

2) The last detective story I read was by Henning Mankell. / I don't read detective stories.

3) Speaking good English gives you all kinds of job opportunities.

4) Fine wine and good company put me in a good mood.

5) I think my dream of living in London might come true.

6) I used to play April fool's jokes when I was a kid but it's something I haven't done for years. / We once played a great April fool's joke on a teacher at school.

7) It's not for me to say what my strong points are.

8) The only old people I have contact with are my grandparents.

Modals

A.

1) He **can't** speak German.

2) We hope to **be able to** go back there next summer.

3) I wish we **could** see each other more often.

4) It **may** snow tomorrow.

5) The exchange rate **might** not be as good next week.

6) Fortunately the rain stopped and I **was able to** finish the job.

7) We **might** easily have lost that match: the other team played really well.

8) You **have** to press that button to start it.

9) She **has to** be at work by 9 o'clock every day.

10) We **don't have** to decide immediately: we have a day or two to think it over.

11) You **mustn't** touch that wire: it's dangerous!

12) You **don't have to** have a car to get around here: the public transport is excellent.

B. Sample Answers

1) I wish I could play the saxophone.

2) At the very least they ought to / should recycle and separate their household waste.

3) I had to be at school/work/university at 8.30 yesterday.

4) We might have all grown up speaking German.

5) I have to do the shopping and go to the post office.

6) No, I wasn't. I made three mistakes.

7) I can't bear the fact that it's more about who you know than what you know.

Negatives

A.

1) **Nobody** has ever spoken to me like that before.

2) All things considered, it was **not** expensive.

3) I'm afraid there will **not** be enough time to go to the other museum.

4) There is **no** indication of how long it will take.

5) **None** of my brothers went to university.

6) **No** referee would have given a penalty for that.

7) I **can't** hear what she is saying.

8) He says he **can't** find it anywhere.

9) I would prefer **not to** go.

10) We had the worst seats in the house: we **couldn't** even see the stage properly.

B.

1) There **was nobody** with us who could speak Chinese.

2) There **is neither a theatre nor** a cinema in the town.

3) They **don't work here any** more.

4) The best strategy is **not to say anything**.

5) I would offer you some cake but unfortunately **there isn't any** / **there is none** left.

Numbers

A.

1) She is one metre, seventy-five tall.

2) The boat is thirty metres long.

3) Lecce is two thousand, three hundred and twenty-two kilometres from London. / London is two thousand, three hundred and twenty-two kilometres from Lecce.

4) The baby weighed three and a half kilos.

5) There are two things she hates.

6) I have only one objection. / I only have one objection

7) She was born on the nineteenth of January, nineteen ninety-two.

B. Sample Answers

1) I'm twenty-nine (years old). / I'm twelve and a half (years old).

2) I'm one metre, sixty-five (centimetres) (tall).

3) My birthday is on the twenty-third of August / on August the twenty-third.

4) I was born in 1992.

5) We usually have dinner about half [past] eight / eight thirty.

6) I think it's about one hundred and thirty thousand.

7) 50% of 3, 000 is 1,500.

Of or 's or nothing

A.

1) Which is your favourite **Shakespeare play / of Shakespeare's plays / play of Shakespeare's**?

2) The road was blocked by a **herd of cows**.

3) How are your **Latin lessons** going?

4) I'm thinking of doing a **yoga course**.

5) It is faster than the **speed of light**.

6) I'm very envious! She has a **month's holiday**.

7) He has an impressive **knowledge of computers**.

8) Some of my best friends are **engineering students / students of engineering**.

9) These animals hibernate during the **winter months**.

10) We're going to a **Springsteen concert** in Milan next month.

11) We went on a school trip to the **Fiat factory** when we were teenagers.

12) My **stomach muscles** are aching after all that exercise.

B. Sample Answers

1) The most interesting tourist destinations near where I live are Pompeii and Vesuvius.

2) The summer months are usually a bit more relaxing than the winter months.

3) My favourite Disney film is "One Hundred and One Dalmatians".

4) I get five weeks' holiday a year.

5) I have written several articles for the university newspaper.

6) My lifestyle has hardly changed at all in the last five years.

7) I think it is vitally important to protect all endangered animal species.

Participles

A.

1) Juventus have only been **beaten** twice so far this season.

2) I want to apologise for not **replying** sooner.

3) Where is the book **set** ?

4) He is not going out much at the moment; he is **concentrating** on preparing his next exam.

5) How long have your parents been **married**?

6) Are you **interested** in modern art?

7) **_Seeing_** as you have time on your hands, you could help me with this.

8) After **_completing_** the course, she found a job immediately.

9) My nephew goes to a school **_specialising_** in classical subjects.

10) Please find **_attached_** my CV.

B. Sample Answers

1) My favourite film is set in New York.

2) Last week I had to apologise for arriving late at a lesson.

3) I went to a school specialising in classical subjects.

4) I'm concentrating as hard as I can.

5) I'm interested in all kinds of things.

Phrasal Verbs

A.

1) I had a row with my girlfriend on the phone and she hung **_up_** on me.

2) The local theatre company is putting **_on_** Macbeth next month.

3) A guy in the street came **_up_** to me and asked me for money.

4) I can't work **_out_** how to open this thing.

5) The children take **_up_** a lot of my time these days.

6) We don't get many holidays but we always go **_away_** for a few days in August.

7) It sounded interesting but it turned **_out_** to be a disappointment.

8) Who do you get **_on_** best with?

9) Giving **_up_** cigarettes was the hardest thing I have ever done.

10) Students have to make **_up_** any lessons they miss.

11) Where do you want me to drop you **_off_**?

12) I'm too busy to take **_on_** any more work at the moment.

B. Sample Answers

1) I get on best with my sister. / I don't get on with anyone.

2) I could never give up football.

3) I'm saving up for a holiday.

4) I am often involved in putting on plays with a theatre company I belong to.

5) I would go back to the Belle Époque or the Renaissance.

6) I drive or walk.

7) We are going away for the weekend at the end of next month.

8) I go out three or four times a week.

Possessives

A.

1) I banged **_my_** head yesterday and it's still hurting me.

2) She suffered regularly from morning sickness during **_her_** pregnancy.

3) I don't think mine is as good as **_yours_**.

4) A colleague of **_ours_** is trying to resolve the problem.

5) Living alone has **_its_** advantages.

6) Can you correct these exercises **_of mine_** / **_for me_**?

7) We were impressed by London and all **_its_** parks.

8) He is saving up to buy **_a house of his own_**.

9) In **_this letter of hers_** she describes the house where she lived.

10) I'm going away for a week but **_on my return_** I will call you.

B. Sample Answers

1) My free time is so limited that I don't do anything.

2) I haven't met mine but most of my friends have met theirs.

3) It's absolutely essential for me to have a house of my own?

4) It's famous for its architecture.

5) No one I know has a life as interesting as mine.

Prepositions

A.

1) She was engaged **_to_** Vito but ended up getting married **_to_** Nicola.

2) The Queen is returning **_to_** London this afternoon and leaving **_for_** Scotland next week.

3) Who has he fallen in love **_with_** this time?

4) She doesn't think much **_of_** the present she got **_from_** her brother-in-law.

5) I've been thinking **_about_** when we first moved **_to_** / **_into_** this house.

6) The boss says she is very satisfied **_with_** my work and I'm happy **_about_** that.

7) You need to do this **_within_** / **_in_** the next three days: **_by_** Saturday at the latest.

8) The film is inspired **_by_** the true story of a woman who sells everything she has **_to_** pay **_for_** medical treatment.

9) She reminds me **_of_** a character **_in_** a film I saw **_at_** the weekend.

10) I asked _____ them **_for_** confirmation that they will all be leaving **_at_** the same time.

11) It depends **_on_** whether you think there is a real need **_for_** it.

12) I read **_in_** a magazine that, **_of_** the two, she was the one more obsessed **_with_** money.

B. Sample Answers

1) I'm feeling pretty good at the moment.

2) The best thing about living in Italy is the quality and variety of the food.

3) My first trip abroad was to Greece.

4) I can't express what I think of him in polite English.

5) I closely identify with the character played by Michael Douglas in "Falling Down".

6) I'm too shy to ask anyone for their autograph. / No, but if I ever meet Lino Banfi, I will definitely ask him for his.

7) I moved into the house I'm living in now about ten years ago.

8) At weekends I catch up on my sleep and go out with friends.

Pronunciations

A.

1) The police report says you were walking when you were supposed to be working.

2) Can you supply the hotel with tubes on the afternoon of Thursday 30th [the thirtieth]?

3) The recipe says to heat it to a low temperature before you eat it.

4) They bought the cupboard for a particular purpose.

5) Our mayor's parents can't bear the women in the village.

6) The engineers considered the techniques mentioned by management.

7) One answer is to control your weight in future.

8) I spilt fruit juice on my suit during the cruise.

9) We honestly thought the unit on the canal would be available.

10) My colleague got his certificate on Tuesday 13th [the thirteenth].

11) The success of the formula was a pure accident.

12) Is it correct that the changes that occurred on the surface were occasional?

B. Sample Answers

1) I'm one metre, sixty five tall and I'm not going to tell you my weight.

2) I sometimes have biscuits but I never have fruit juice for breakfast.

3) We were taught Italian and English literature at school.

4) I'm extremely concerned about the earth and the environment.

5) My favourite building in the world is the Colosseum.

6) For the moment I haven't thought through my plans for the future very thoroughly.

7) I consider my colleagues as honest as the day is long.

8) The worst thing that's happened in Italy recently is the economic crisis.

Questions

A.

1) What **are** you doing tomorrow evening?

2) How long have you **been** living in Catania?

3) How many times have you been **to** Venice?

4) You're Italian, aren't **you**?

5) How **do** you get to work?

6) How do I **go** about getting a new passport?

B.

1) Who is it?

2) Where are you from? / Where do you come from?

3) Has she [got] a car? / Does she ~~has~~ have a car?

4) What time did she leave the office?

5) What happened?

6) How many people came?

7) What does "mistake" mean?

8) How tall is he?

Redundant Word

A.

1) When I was seven ~~years~~, my parents divorced.

2) Our house is three kilometres ~~far~~ from the sea.

3) I like the sea but my girlfriend prefers ~~more~~ the mountains.

4) She is studying Chinese ~~language~~.

5) He continued playing despite ~~of~~ his injury.

6) They gave ~~to~~ me a gift voucher for my birthday.

7) You will need ~~of~~ more than one.

8) What time are you going ~~to~~ home this evening?

9) We would like to discuss ~~about~~ this problem with a lawyer.

10) She is saving up ~~for~~ to pay for a training course.

11) Her parents are ~~two~~ teachers.

12) Their son, Marco, ~~he~~ is an engineer.

B.

1) How far is the town where you live ~~distant~~ from the sea?

2) What kinds of things do you tend not to discuss ~~about~~ with your family?

3) What team do you support ~~for~~?

4) What ~~the~~ languages have you studied?

5) Are you studying English ~~for~~ to improve your job prospects or for other reasons?

C. Sample Answers

1) It's about twenty kilometres from the sea. / It's not far at all from the sea.

2) I tend not to discuss my relationship problems.

3) I support Sampdoria.

4) I have studied German, Swedish and Ancient Greek.

5) To improve my job prospects.

Reflexives

A.

*1) Look after **yourself**!*

*2) Did you **enjoy yourselves**?*

*3) We first **met** at university.*

*4) You should try to **relax** more.*

*5) I get the impression you don't like talking about **yourself**.*

*6) They **got to know each other** quite well over the following weeks.*

*7) His parents **separated** when he was still a toddler.*

*8) We **haven't seen each other** since primary school.*

*9) Readers will not find it easy to **identify** with the hero of the story.*

*10) She is going to **graduate** next July.*

*11) They are always arguing **with** each other.*

*12) Our plan is to **marry** some time next year.*

B. Sample Answers

1) I last really enjoyed myself at a party a couple of weeks ago.

2) I suppose I might marry / get married one day.

3) I like to relax by walking in the mountains.

4) I try not to talk about myself too much.

5) Two of my sisters argue all the time.

Relatives

A.

*1) e) I have a very good friend **who works in Pavia**.*

*2) g) Have you met the guys [that] **she has hired to do the job**?*

3) **h)** *Anyone who requires a vegetarian meal* **should let us know beforehand**.

4) **k)** *In the photo there is a baby* **crawling across a lawn**.

5) **c)** *My parents would prefer* **me to stay in Italy**.

6) **a)** *There's a very good reason* **why we ask you to do this**.

7) **d)** *We're looking for a place* **to do up ourselves**.

8) **i)** *This is the very house* **where he was born**.

9) **f)** *She can't decide* **what she wants**.

10) **j)** *Have you any idea* **whose jacket this is?**

11) **b)** *They are talking about politics,* **which is something I hate**.

B. Sample Answers

1) *I tend not to say what I think when doing so might get me into trouble.*

2) *I can recommend a number of places to spend a relaxing weekend.*

3) *The first TV series [that] I saw in English was "Peppa Pig".*

4) *The people [that] I can always ask for help are my family and my best friend.*

5) *The reason [why] I'm reading this book is that I make a lot of mistakes in English!*

6) *I would like / would have liked my teachers to spend less time on admin and more time with us students.*

Singular & Plural Forms

A.

1) *Most people* **don't** *like that kind of thing.*

2) *I have been* **friends** *with him for many years.*

3) *It was one of the scariest* **experiences** *I have ever had.*

4) *Have you been to any* **concerts** *recently?*

5) *I was a very active* **child**.

6) *She is a* **fan** *of Madonna.*

7) *How many* **DVDs** *did you lend her?*

8) *People are always leaving their* **umbrellas** *on the bus.*

9) *None of the* **other** *students passed the exam.*

10) *Our mission is simply to feed the* **hungry**.

11) *They own a* **five-metre** *boat.*

12) *The association meets every* **Wednesday**.

B. Sample Answers

1) *I hardly ever buy DVDs?*

2) *Politics doesn't interest me at all.*

3) On Sundays I rarely get up before ten.

4) I own three pairs of jeans.

5) I have never caught any fish because I have never been fishing. / I caught three trout on holiday last year.

6) A lot of the people in the town where I live are rather narrow-minded.

Some & Any

A.

1) Are there **any** rivers in Puglia?

2) That cake looks delicious! Can I have **some**?

3) This cheese is really good. **Would you like some**?

4) We could spend **a few** hours looking round that art gallery you mentioned.

5) A spokesman said that **a number of** candidates were being considered for the post.

6) For the most part it's a very civilised place although you do meet some rude **people**.

7) Have you seen any good **films** recently?

8) The show was amazing: she is **some** singer!

9) **Some use** garlic in this recipe but we prefer it without.

10) There are **several** reasons why you can't go: firstly you're too young, secondly it's too expensive and thirdly it's dangerous.

B. Sample Answers

1) I haven't had time to plan any holidays.

2) I would love to spend a few hours with Natalie Portman.

3) If I had any, I wouldn't admit it.

4) The only people that can call me any time are my family.

5) If I were going to give some advice to tourists visiting my town, I would suggest they just wander around.

Spellings

A.

1) address   2) beautiful   3) believe   4) constant   5) grandparents
6) healthy   7) studying   8) thanks   9) theatre   10) which

B.

1) August   2) breakfast   3) developed   4) exam   5) fabulous
6) imagine   7) month   8) peaceful   9) teacher   10) tolerant

C.

1) choice   2) comfortable   3) difficult   4) enjoyed   5) especially   6) independence

7) mystery   8) participate   9) philosophy   10) psychology   11) something

D.

1) bicycle   2) character   3) Michael   4) physical   5) together   6) with

Tenses: Present

A.

1) One of my former students now **lives** in Liverpool.

2) Her children **don't** eat meat.

3) What time does your lesson **finish**?

4) **Do you** agree with the proposal?

5) I **am writing** to you to inform you that I wish to end my subscription.

6) Why **are you looking** at me like that? **Is my face** dirty?

7) She **can't** see very well without her glasses.

8) Can you ask her what **she wants**?

9) We **usually** spend a month there in the summer.

B. Sample Answers

1) From my bedroom window I can see the apartment building across the street.

2) I can't hear my neighbours but I can hear their horrible music.

3) I'm enjoying life as much as anyone can with exams to prepare for.

4) I usually spend my holidays trying to entertain my children.

5) I have no idea what my best friend is doing right now. / She's probably shopping.

6) I don't entirely disagree with the idea but it needs to be thought through properly.

Tenses: Future Forms

A.

1) It will be difficult if you **don't get** someone to help you.

2) You will be informed when your documents **are** ready.

3) As soon as we **hear** from the lawyer, we will let you know.

4) We **are meeting** some friends in the Irish pub at half past eight this evening.

5) I think I**'ll do** it now. I won't have time later.

6) She **is going** / **is going to go** back to Taranto to see her parents next weekend.

7) Don't worry: I **will not be** / **won't be** angry if you don't finish in time.

B. Sample Answers

1) Some friends are coming from Rome to stay with me.

2) This time next year I think I'll still be here. / I hope I'll be abroad somewhere.

3) I'm going to take things easy while I examine my options.

4) If I get any free time this week, I will probably spend it sleeping.

Tenses: Simple Past

A.

1) She **wasn't** at school yesterday.

2) My father **taught** in a secondary school for twenty years.

3) I **found** my watch in the pocket of my other jacket.

4) The wedding **cost** them a fortune.

5) He **died** before he finished composing his last symphony.

6) We **chose** it because it seemed the best option at the time.

7) They both **had** great difficulty understanding what he was saying.

8) We didn't **manage** to get there in time.

9) Where did you **buy** it?

10) When I was eleven, I **started** doing guitar lessons.

11) The last film I **saw** at the cinema was "Interstellar".

12) My friend used to **come** to my house every evening after school.

B.

1) Things **became** easier as time went by.

2) We **began** going out together three and a half years ago.

3) Who **gave** you permission to do that?

4) What time **did you get** home last night?

5) My nose used to **bleed** every time I went up a mountain.

6) At the time I **thought** it was strange.

7) They **were** both born in Abruzzo.

8) It's time we **left**.

9) We **lived** there for eight years but then we **moved**.

10) At the age of fifteen, I **joined** a band.

C. Sample Answers

1) I don't actually know where my best friend was born. / He was born somewhere near Naples.

2) We used to do sport twice a week at primary school.

3) I can't remember what the last book I read was. / It was a novel by a Portuguese author.

4) I had a canary for a year or two but it died.

5) I was four and a half when I started school.

Tenses: Present Perfect & Past Perfect

A.

1) She **has** become a first-rate photographer.

2) **Have** the invitations all been sent out?

3) I **have had** this teddy bear since I was three.

4) He has made excellent progress **this month**.

5) Is it the first time you **have done** anything like this?

6) I **hadn't** eaten sea urchins before we tried them in that restaurant.

7) We **have been going** there for years: we love the place!

8) There isn't any ice cream left because your sister **has** eaten it all.

9) They **had** never been up a volcano until we took them to Etna.

10) If she **had** arrived earlier, she could have eaten with us.

11) I **realised** too late what I had done.

12) My mother thought my father had **forgotten** but he **hadn't**.

B. Sample Answers

1) I have lived in my house since I was born. / I have lived in my house for fifteen years.

2) I haven't spent very much money this month.

3) I have been working on this exercise for about five minutes.

4) I have done a number of jobs in the last few years.

5) If I hadn't decided to study English today, I would have spent the time decluttering my room.

Tenses: Conditionals

A.

1) **c)** When I finish university, I would **like to become a journalist**.

2) **a)** You really should **have been honest with me from the start**.

3) **i)** I was happy at that school and would **have preferred not to move**.

4) **f)** She would like to get **married in a country church**.

5) **l)** We were afraid that he **would not agree to the proposal**.

6) **k)** I think I'd like **to wait a little longer before making a final decision**.

7) **j)** If you had followed my advice, this **would never have happened**.

8) **b)** My grandfather always said that it **would never happen**.

9) **h)** *If I had had any idea what was going on, I **would have done something about it.***

10) **g)** *I wish the **weather would improve.***

11) **d)** *Did you think it **would be easier?***

12) **e)** *I know I shouldn't **eat this kind of thing but it's so tempting.***

B. Sample Answers

1) *I would most like to live somewhere civilised, like Stockholm or Vancouver.*

2) *If I can't sleep tonight, I'll read my book.*

3) *I imagined I would be a train driver.*

4) *If I weren't here now, I'd be out with my friends.*

5) *I would have chosen somewhere they speak English, like Australia or New Zealand.*

6) *They should start by cutting their own salaries.*

Transitive or Intransitive

A.

1) **l)** *He is living **the life of Riley.***

2) **k)** *The built-in flash allows **you to use the camera even in poor lighting.***

3) **c)** *They dismissed **him for inappropriate behaviour.***

4) **i)** *Last night I dreamed **about the demonstration.***

5) **b)** *She prefers to wear **casual clothes.***

6) **e)** *There's an emergency meeting to discuss **the proposed strike action.***

7) **g)** *She quit **after they increased the working hours.***

8) **f)** *This kind of initiative encourages **people to use their cars less.***

9) **a)** *We are having **a difficult time.***

10) **h)** *They always dress **the baby in blue.***

11) **j)** *We have been experimenting **with different kinds of food.***

12) **d)** *Caesar ordered **it to be done that same day.***

B. Sample Answers

1) *I dreamed about when I was a child. / I can't remember what I dreamed about.*

2) *I usually suggest foreign visitors try pizza and tiramisu first.*

3) *I wear a tracksuit or pyjamas around the house.*

4) *I experience difficult situations all the time.*

5) *I can't tell you very much, I'm afraid.*

6) *Schools should not allow students to use mobile phones in the classroom.*

Word Order

A.

1) I have three **other** cousins in Basilicata.

2) **You** have a great holiday too!

3) She would like to get to know her in-laws **better**.

4) Do you know where **they** are?

5) It would be great to spend a couple of weeks **together**.

6) Do you remember how **small** the portions were in that restaurant?

7) Only when the dish is almost ready, **should** you add the cheese on top.

8) We are going to begin the renovation work **soon**.

9) I had never seen **such** a dilapidated building.

10) She's the one person who I know will always be **there** for me.

11) Try that number **again**.

12) You should contact your nearest police station **immediately**. / You should **immediately** contact your nearest police station.

B.

1) We enjoyed the holiday very much.

2) My sister is teaching me to play the piano.

3) They are slowly restoring the facade.

4) She doesn't allow anyone to touch it.

5) The book is certainly worth reading.

6) It was quite a frightening experience.

7) We remember the occasion with pleasure.

8) I remember when I saw snow for the first time.

9) He likes it too much to give it up.

10) She got a beautiful new pair of earrings for her birthday.

C. Sample Answers

1) I don't enjoy studying English very much. / I enjoy studying English quite a lot.

2) For my last birthday I got some CDs and a gift voucher.

3) If I had a Ferrari, I wouldn't allow anyone to drive it!

4) I don't really have a favourite TV series.

5) At my school, when the teachers weren't there, it was chaos.

6) I would say that "La grande bellezza" and "Mia madre" are the ones most worth watching.

7) I think Heaven exists only in the imagination.

8) My youngest relative was born at the beginning of last year.

9) I must have been five or six when I first rode a bicycle.

10) It looks great! / To be honest, I didn't even notice you'd had it cut. / You call that a haircut?

Wrong Word

A.

1) She always wears very **colourful** clothes.

2) The book tells the **story** of a man who is obsessed with the **history** of 20th century Germany.

3) The **journey** from the airport to the hotel was a nightmare but apart from that it was a great **trip**.

4) I first **met** him at church and he struck me as very honest but then I **found out** from his ex-wife that he had had a number of **affairs** behind her back.

5) My husband loves living in Cambridge and I don't think he would **agree** to **move** to a smaller **town**.

6) I studied science **subjects** at school but I've forgotten **everything**.

7) We had a **coffee** in a **café** a couple of **blocks** away from the railway station.

8) He's a great **cook**: even his **mashed** potatoes taste like heaven.

9) She is **looking for** an excuse not to tell the other **members** of her family about it.

10) I'll **join** you in Paris on Wednesday and then **take** you on to London with me at the weekend.

11) It's the kind of work that **requires imagination** and an ability to think outside the **box**.

12) The characters in the film are all **well-constructed** and the **performances** by the two leading actors are magnificent.

B.

1) He had the **opportunity** to go and work in San Francisco but he turned it down.

2) These schools provide students with an excellent **education**.

3) I haven't yet **achieved** all my objectives.

4) Her **explanation** of how it works couldn't have been clearer.

5) He is still trying to come to terms with his wife's **betrayal**.

6) The idea is to **prevent** smugglers bringing drugs into the country.

7) They were **obliged** by circumstances to sell up and move.

8) She retired from public life and is now living in a quiet **suburb** of Milan.

9) Is it a method you would **recommend** to other students?

10) These events undoubtedly played a part in **shaping** his personality.

C. Sample Answers

1) I have moved house three times.

2) The things that most remind me of my childhood are the smell of cut grass and the taste of my mother's apple pie.

3) I would most like to go back to the west coast of Ireland

4) I have been commuting to work for the last five years.

5) Most of the other members of my family speak English better than me.

6) I once acted in an amateur production of "Hamlet".

7) I'm most anxious to get a job in my field of study.

8) I usually get together with my family about once a week.

9) My favourite subjects at school were physics and chemistry.

10) I was obliged to pay the television licence fee even though I never watch TV.

ACKNOWLEDGEMENTS

The author would like to thank the following people for their help: Silvia Capursi, both for her technical advice and for her suggestions regarding the Italian used in the book; Valeria Marangio and Antonella Ranieri from the *Centro Linguistico* at the Polytechnic of Bari for their extremely helpful observations regarding content and layout (I am also indebted to Valeria for her ingenious idea of including a mistake in the title); Mark and Alicia Marone for their very useful input on contemporary American usage; Noemi De Nicolò for her invaluable proof-reading; Iris De Nicolò for not complaining about me monopolising the computer; all those friends, acquaintances, students, colleagues and strangers who have, however inadvertently, contributed raw materials to this book.

KINDLE VERSION

English Mistakes Italians ~~Do~~ Make is also available in electronic format for Kindle, iPad, iPhone, smartphone, PC, etc from all amazon sites.

ABOUT THE AUTHOR

Paul Andrew Jarvis was born and educated in Birkenhead, England. His first English teaching experience was in Pau, France, where from 1984-1985 he worked as a language assistant at the Lycée Louis Barthou and the Collège du Bois d'Amour. After graduating from the University of Sheffield in 1986 with a degree in French Language and Literature, he spent two years teaching English to students in the Arts, Law and Science faculties of the University of Le Mans, in France. In 1989 he obtained a Post-Graduate Teaching Certificate in Modern Languages from Goldsmiths' College, University of London, before moving to Italy, where he taught EFL at Lord Byron College and the British School. For the past 24 years he has taught English at the Faculty of Arts (now LELIA) at the University of Bari, and since the year 2000 he has also been lecturing at the Polytechnic of Bari. In addition, he has worked as a freelance translator, writes a monthly column for English language students in the online newspaper *da BITONTO* and is the author of a number of books.

OTHER BOOKS BY THE SAME AUTHOR

English Language

1000 Real Answers – English Phrasebook & Self-Study Guide, Createspace, 2012

1000 Real Answers – English Phrasebook, Createspace, 2013

English Grammar Crosswords, Createspace, 2014

Bilingual Books for Children

Misery Puss – Micio Musone, Extremathule Edizioni, 2009 (co-authored with Claudia la Viola)

Jimmy Squirrel & The Crazy Market – Jimmy Scoiattolo e il mercato matto, Createspace, 2013 (co-authored with Silvia Rita Capursi)

Jimmy Squirrel & The Crazy Market – Jimmy Eichhörnchen Und Der Verrückte Markt, Createspace, 2013 (co-authored with Silvia Rita Capursi; translated by Julia Wachenfeld)

Novel

Dio non sta bene, Le Bolle Blu Edizioni, 2010 (translated from the English by Angela Castellano). Published in English as *The Wooden-Legged Elephant*, Createspace, 2012.

Printed in Poland
by Amazon Fulfillment
Poland Sp. z o.o., Wrocław

50786197R00125